INNOVATIVE
PERFORMANCE
SUPPORT

INNOVATIVE PERFORMANCE SUPPORT

Strategies and Practices for Learning in the Workflow

Conrad Gottfredson, Ph.D.
Bob Mosher

New York   Chicago   San Francisco   Lisbon   London
Madrid   Mexico City   Milan   New Delhi   San Juan
Seoul   Singapore   Sydney   Toronto

4 5 6 7 8 9 10 QVS/QVS 19 18 17 16 15

ISBN 978-0-07-170311-6
MHID 0-07-170311-X

This publication is designed to provide accurate and authoritative information in regard to the subject matter covered. It is sold with the understanding that neither the author nor the publisher is not engaged in rendering legal, accounting, securities trading, or other professional services. If legal advice or other expert assistance is required, the services of a competent professional person should be sought.
—From a Declaration of Principles Jointly Adopted by a Committee of the American Bar Association and a Committee of Publishers and Associations

Library of Congress Cataloging-in-Publication
Gottfredson, Conrad.
  Innovative performance support : tools and strategies for learning in the workflow / by Conrad Gottfredson, Bob Mosher.
    p. cm.
  ISBN 978-0-07-170311-6 (alk. paper)
  1. Performance technology. 2. Employees—Training of. I. Mosher, Bob. II. Title.
  HF5549.5.P37G68 2011
  658.3'124—dc22

                    2010032037

Product or brand names used in this book may be trade names or trademarks. Where we believe that there may be proprietary claims to such trade names or trademarks, the name has been used with an initial capital or it has been capitalized in the style used by the name claimant. Regardless of the capitalization used, all such names have been used in an editorial manner without any intent to convey endorsement of or other affiliation with the name claimant. Neither the author nor the publisher intends to express any judgment as to the validity or legal status of any such proprietary claims.

McGraw-Hill books are available at special quantity discounts to use as premiums and sales promotions or for use in corporate training programs. To contact a representative, please e-mail us at bulksales@mcgraw-hill.com.

This book is printed on acid-free paper.

Contents

Foreword

by Elliott Masie

I n 2007, the MASIE Center invited Bob Mosher and Conrad Gottfredson to develop and facilitate an intensive three-day workshop
on Performance Support. Our motivation was to extend the toolkit
and competencies of learning professionals in large, global organizations, to more effectively support the performance of workers on
the job. Not a new idea, but a glaring gap in the world of instructional design. Although this notion of Performance Support has
been around for a long time, we saw a need to focus attention back
on this discipline and update its practices to address the challenging
needs of twenty-first-century learners.

Today there are four very different generations working together:
traditionalists (born before 1946), baby boomers (born 1946 to
1964), Generation Xers (born 1965 to 1981), and millennials (born
1980s to 2000.) The differences in how they approach learning certainly call for an upgrade to the way we support them. We are finding that all of these generations are seeking greater autonomy in

their work processes, while wanting to have more rapid pathways to competency and excellence.

Work environments are also in a state of constant upheaval, which has increased the demand for Performance Support. The good news is that there are enabling technologies that can help. What's needed are updated practices to address all of this. With this in mind, we challenged Con and Bob to establish practical solutions for today's Performance Support environment. They did just that, and this book is the result of that work.

They see their mission as one of "performer support." Their first response to any need for employee performance improvement is to focus first on the "moment of Apply" and then wrap other learning support around the performer support solutions they develop. The result? They are demonstrating with hard metrics the positive impact of their efforts on employee performance. Managers at all levels, especially front-line managers, have assumed greater ownership of learning at all five moments of need (that is, when learning for the first time, when learning more, when applying and remembering, when solving problems, and when things change.)

More importantly, people throughout the organization have become more agile in how they learn. They are learning, unlearning, and relearning more rapidly. They have become more self-directed, adaptive, and collaborative in how they go about their day-to-day learning.

If this is what you want for your organization, then this book is written for you. It is much more than a must read. It merits study and implementation. I've known the authors for most of their professional careers. They have walked the talk. This book does a great job in talking that walk.

Introduction

IT SHOULD ALWAYS HAVE BEEN ABOUT APPLY

What we have to learn to do, we learn by doing.

—*Aristotle*

Our industry has made great progress in meeting the instructional needs of people who are learning something for the first time and when they want to learn more. We have rightly broadened our approach from the traditional classroom to include other formal means to help people learn quickly and effectively. We have employed innovative technologies to make these learning opportunities available anywhere, any time. We are, for the most part, very good at focused, event-based learning—synchronous and asynchronous.

But on the whole, we have been negligent in addressing the most critical moment in any person's individual learning process: his or her moment of "Apply." Preparing learners for this vital moment should have always been at the heart of our efforts. This is when learners meet the realities of what they actually learned, what they didn't learn, what they have forgotten, and what they have misunderstood. They confront the unanticipated nuances and the challenge of a constantly changing performance landscape.

Years ago, while demonstrating an emerging technology to an advanced instructional design class (a technology that would literally coach people through a software procedure while they did their work), an aspiring instructional designer raised his hand and asked, "What about practice?" Now, this wasn't simply simulation software. With this technology users could invoke a script that communicated directly with the operating system and the application. The script would literally walk a person through a software procedure a step at a time, allowing the person to use her own data to literally do her own work.

When the student was asked, "Why would you need practice if this helps someone actually do his work?" he responded, "You have to have practice to learn." He was unable to shake the formal learning event paradigm from his mindset. He was absolutely ignorant of his core mission: to develop learning solutions that ensure that people can perform effectively when they are called upon to act. He needed to put and keep his sights squarely on the "moment of Apply." So do all of us. In the past we might have been able to ignore this vital moment and still somehow stumble on into successful performance, but the nature of the world today won't let us do that. It demands that we focus squarely on Apply.

What is more, today's work environment doesn't tolerate learners stepping out of their workflow to learn unless it is absolutely vital to do so. And the actual nature of twenty-first-century learners is resistant to learning options that are delayed and removed from the here and now. They are self-directed, adaptive, and collaborative in their approach to learning. These kind of learners will ultimately abandon outright our formal learning solutions if what we provide them fails to efficiently prepare them to effectively perform at their moments of Apply. Why? Because when facing a traditional course that fails to do this, today's learners are predisposed to simply walk away and look elsewhere for the shortest path to Apply.

Responding to this need, of course, is the core calling of Performance Support. Its primary mission is to support people at the critical moment of Apply. The good news is that doing this doesn't require more effort than what most are doing now. It does, however, require a mindset shift. It also necessitates our learning how to redirect current efforts to bring about this alignment.

We aren't proposing the overthrow of formal learning events. But we are advocating that we move much of what we do as far into the natural workflow of the organization as possible, that we avoid, when we can, pulling people from their work for large periods of time to learn. There has never been a time when we have had greater capacity to do this than now.

In *The Sun Also Rises*, Ernest Hemingway's character, when asked how he had gone bankrupt, replies: "First gradually, and then suddenly." This will be the case for much of what we call formal learning today—unless we push our efforts more deeply into the organizational workflow and provide people the tools and preparation they need to successfully perform at the moment of Apply. This must be at the heart of all we do. It should always have been the case.

INNOVATIVE
PERFORMANCE
SUPPORT

1

THE CASE FOR PERFORMANCE SUPPORT

In a time of drastic change, it is the learners who inherit the future. The learned usually find themselves equipped to live in a world that no longer exists. [1]

—*Eric Hoffer, American social writer*

A STORY TO GET STARTED: THE MINNOWS, FROM BOB

My father ran a summer camp as part of his work with the YMCA. During one of those camps I was given the assignment with a friend to teach the Minnows how to swim. The Minnows were the youngest nonswimmers in camp. On that first morning of instruction, they all lined up along the edge of the pool. I was in the water with my teaching partner when, without warning, he reached up, grabbed one of the Minnows, and tossed him into the pool. The kid quickly popped to the surface and started flailing around, taking in water. My training buddy then put a hand under the terrorized child and guided him along the surface, with his little minnow arms flailing away, back to the edge of the pool. Then he lifted him up onto the edge of the pool where no other Minnow remained standing. They had all backed as far away from the pool's edge as possible.

I stood in the water in shock. This wasn't how I had envisioned the swimming instruction to go. Still dumbfounded, I asked, "What are you doing?" He responded, "Bob, we've only got a week!" My friend realized something that I hadn't. He was focused on the reality that we had only one week to help those kids be safe from drowning. I was caught up in the instructional plan while he was responding to the realities of "time to performance."

Time to performance is defined as the total time required to help a person achieve successful performance. In this Minnow story, it was the week that those Minnows were in camp, and the minimum performance, for them, was "surfacing and making it back to the edge of the pool."

Today, organizations are threatened by a churning pool of constant, unpredictable change. The time to performance required to stay competitive has never been shorter. This abbreviated timeline demands that Performance Support (learning at the moment of "Apply") become the centerpiece of all our efforts in the vital cause of learning. This chapter is written to help you make the case for doing this.

WHAT YOU NEED TO KNOW

In 2008, we saw a financial tsunami hit the United States. The rippling effect is still being felt throughout the world as organizations continue to struggle in how they respond to the clear and present danger of volatile change. The consequences of the inability to adapt at or above the speed of change have wreaked financial havoc since.

Ian Davis, McKinsey's worldwide managing director, has since written the following:

> The business landscape has changed fundamentally; tomorrow's environment will be different, but no less rich in possibilities for those who are prepared. It is increasingly clear that the current downturn is fundamentally different from recessions of

recent decades. We are experiencing not merely another turn of the business cycle, but a restructuring of the economic order.

For some organizations, near-term survival is the only agenda item. Others are peering through the fog of uncertainty, thinking about how to position themselves once the crisis has passed and things return to normal. The question is, "What will normal look like?" While no one can say how long the crisis will last, what we find on the other side will not look like the normal of recent years. The **new normal** will be shaped by a confluence of powerful forces, some arising directly from the financial crisis and some that were at work long before it began.[2]

In the midst of this "New Normal" described by Davis, keeping current in learning is like changing a tire on a moving truck—hence the need for learners to be rapid, adaptive, collaborative, and self-directed. Such dynamic learners thrive most when they have the support they need at the moment of Apply. No organization can adequately meet the challenge of ever-present change without an intentional Performance Support strategy in place and functioning effectively. In the broadest definition, Performance Support (PS) consists of the practices and tools the organization provides its people individually and collectively for them to perform their work successfully and efficiently.

The Value of Performance Support

The proper implementation of these practices and tools can produce a measurable impact for good. Here are some of those impact areas.

PS Delivers Greater Business Efficiencies

Learning leaders have struggled long and hard to link measurable business results to learners who attend some form of formal instruction, in class or online. Why has this been so hard? Why do so many still find this exercise exhausting, expensive, and often inconclusive at a meaningful level?

The answer is in the fundamental flaw in the way that the correlation between a training event and improved business outcomes is measured. There is a huge gap between mastering content delivered in a learning event and being able to apply that content in an effective and productive way on the job. The pursuit of the return on investment (ROI) in the formal training environment has been a bad fit from the start, and without stepping into the Performance Support arena, training will continue to have a difficult, if not impossible time, tying itself to compelling ROI metrics. For example, in the formal training ROI model, we can fairly measure the following:

- Knowledge gain
- Certification
- Demonstrable skill recall
- Compliance

But when an organization ventures into the full range of Performance Support practices now available (with its tools, strategies, and frameworks that complement training), we can begin to effectively measure the following:

- Productivity gains
- Decreases in time to proficiency
- Reductions in support costs
- Completion of job-related tasks
- Increases in user adoption
- Optimized business processes
- Increases in customer satisfaction
- Reductions in transaction costs
- Reductions in implementation costs

The reason we can do this is that the ROI manifests itself in the workflow and on the job. Until training departments design, deliver, and maintain learning strategies that extend into the workflow (that is, until they incorporate Performance Support), calculating the ROI will remain a frustrating and often futile exercise.

PS Promotes Retention and Transfer

If organizations want to maximize their return on their formal learning investment, they will achieve it only via Performance Support. PS bridges the time gap between what is learned during formal learning and the moment when people are called to act upon what they learned. The first part of this bridge is *retention*. Much of what is absorbed during formal training is dead on arrival when learners are finally called upon to perform using that learning in their work. Unfortunately, the reality of knowledge and skill loss is all too clear. The good news, though, is that Performance Support can rapidly resurrect it all, as long as it is designed and implemented properly.

The other half of this bridge between the formal learning and the actual performance on the job is the looming challenge of "transfer." *Transfer* is defined as the capacity of learners to apply what they have learned to the unique environment and moment-to-moment circumstances of work life. Obviously, if there is limited transfer from formal learning to the workflow, the investment in training is squandered. Performance Support plays the key role in ensuring that this doesn't happen and that there is a high-yield return on an organization's investment in formal learning.

PS Expands Knowledge Capacity

Once upon a time, a long time ago, people actually knew everything they needed to know to do their work. Hard to comprehend in today's work environment where people are continually being asked to learn at or above the speed of change and at a time when the information pool we're all drinking from is growing at breakneck speed.

To illustrate: In 2003, Chevron's CIO reported that his company accumulated data at the rate of 2 terabytes—17,592,000,000,000 bits—a day. According to research conducted by the International Data Corporation (IDC), the world created 161 exabytes of data in 2006. That's "3 million times the amount of information contained in all the books ever written." In 2009, the size of the world's total digital content was estimated at 500 billion gigabytes, or 500 exabytes. And it has been predicted that by the end of 2010, we will have generated more than 988 exabytes.[3]

This same pace of information growth is occurring within the individual work requirements of people. Clearly, today people can't store in their internal knowledge base what they need to know to do their work. It's all too vast and fluid. The role of PS is to provide intuitive access to that information in the form needed at the moment of need.

The New Blend:
Making Possible a Complete Learning Ecosystem

Most organizations have two disparate learning arms: a formal learning arm where individual members of the organization learn in the context of specially designed learning events in all their appropriate forms and an informal learning arm where individual members of the organization learn in their workflow at their moment of need in the way they choose to learn. Historically these two arms have functioned separately. Traditionally, the formal learning arm hasn't known nor particularly cared about what the informal learning arm was doing. And the informal learning arm has done its own thing, often struggling to integrate what's learned formally into its informal learning paths.

Figure 1.1 shows these two learning paths. The vertical lines represent the formal learning classes a person might take over a period of time (with that person's path being represented by the arrow in the center of the graphic). As you can see, this individual has taken quite a few courses during these four years. But this person has also been learning in the workflow. The horizontal lines in the figure represent those times when project work and work responsibilities

Figure 1.1. The Relationship between Formal Learning Events and Informal Learning Paths

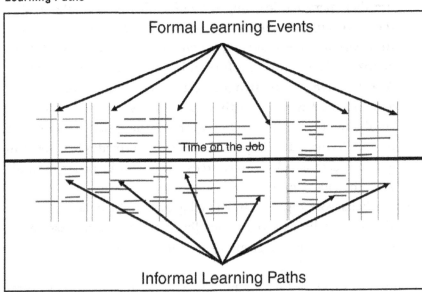

required or fostered learning. Experience is life's greatest teacher, especially when there are challenges including failure.

As you can see, some of the informal learning lines intersect with the formal events (instructor-led classes, e-learning courses, webinars, and so on). The pressing question is: To what degree do the formal courses blend with the informal learning taking place in the person's own workflow?

The good news is that this is happening today. The New Normal is fostering a "New Blend" of formal learning opportunities with intentional informal learning practices. Here's one example of what this kind of blending looks like:

The New Blend Example 1

- Work group members complete self-tailored prework prior to attending a virtual class.
- They attend four virtual meetings each lasting 2.5 hours spread out over eight weeks.

- Following each virtual meeting, learners independently complete "expand" assignments—that is, assignments requiring them to use their personal learning network to learn more about what they were taught during each virtual session. They document what they learn in the expand assignment in a course wiki. (See http:// en.wikipedia.org/wiki/ for further information about a wiki.)
- Also following each virtual meeting, learners complete Apply activities tied directly to their personal work and submit the results to their trainer. They work on these activities using a digital Performance Support broker that provides learners fingertip access to all the resources they need in order to apply what they have learned.
- Students work together in virtual groups to help each other.
- The trainer holds a virtual feedback and coaching session for each set of Apply assignments for each learner.

This New Blend of formal and informal learning practices represents a significant scope shift for training professionals. We are now

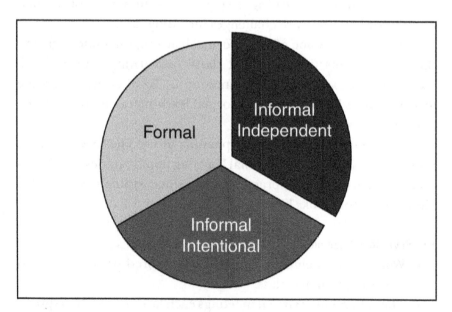

Figure 1.2. The Distinction between Intentional and Independent Informal Learning

intentionally stepping into the informal side of learning. We should have always been doing this, but emerging technologies make it more feasible. Support services and technical publication groups should *not* feel threatened by these efforts. They have much to offer here. But there is more that the training profession can and should be doing in addition.

In reality, the distinction between formal and informal learning should look like the pie chart in Figure 1.2. Formal learning, of course, is what training groups have traditionally done: they build, deliver, and manage learning solutions to support organizational needs.

Informal learning, as you can see in the figure, can be divided into two areas: informal intentional and informal independent. *Informal independent* is learning that individuals and teams may choose to do outside what is planned, implemented, and managed by the training arm of the organization. This has been the elephant in the room for a long time. It's estimated that two-thirds of learning taking place within most organizations has been happening in the informal independent area.

It is readily apparent that there is a greater amount of learning going on outside the formal training we have so adeptly put in place. The reality is that the informal side of learning is where real learning occurs because it is happening in the workflow. However, the costs to organizations when informal learning goes wrong can be staggering. At the very least, informal learning can prove costly through inefficiencies. The root cause of these inefficiencies is the disconnect between formal and informal learning.

The good news is that the New Normal is pushing organizations to become much more intentional in the informal learning area and to blend those intentional practices with formal learning. This New Blend looks something like this:

The New Blend Example 2

- An employee is in the middle of a pressing multimonth work project. She consults her digital Performance Support broker and identifies four areas where there are unique twists that require additional knowledge and skills to complete the project successfully.

- She immediately accesses directly from her broker, several microblogs where she shares her learning need out through several follower groups (internal and external to the company).
- A representative from the learning group, along with other microbloggers, immediately provides recommendations. She sorts through those recommendations and does the following:
  o Schedules and takes three recommended e-learning courses, two from within the company's Learning Management System (LMS) and one purchased independently from an independent e-university.
  o Schedules and participates in four virtual coaching sessions—two internally sponsored and two from a colleague-friend from another company.
  o Skims through three books: one hard-copy book, one digital book purchased online, and one digital book accessed from a free Web site.
- As she moves forward to complete the project, she frequently accesses her electronic Performance Support broker to guide her as she and her team complete each critical task.
- After she completes the project, she takes 10 minutes and accesses a "lessons learned" template, via the Performance Support broker, in which she briefly documents the lessons she learned. She enriches it with metadata, posts it, and then pushes it out to her direct manager as part of her project report.

As you can see, there is a blend of formal learning solutions (for example, e-learning courses, virtual coaching sessions), independent informal learning (for example, scanning through books), and intentional informal learning (using the Performance Support broker to gain access to the resources she needs at her moments of Apply).

Performance Support is the discipline that harnesses informal learning and makes it intentional. Performance Support includes the practices and tools an organization provides its people individually and collectively to enable them to perform their work efficiently.

Here's how this New Blend of formal and informal intentional learning benefits an organization:

- Without intentional support, informal learning can be unruly and therefore costly. Unconsciously, incompetent people often help others become the same. A strong Performance Support infrastructure counters this.

- Most performers work in an environment where their skill sets are in a state of continual flux. Performance Support delivers intentional capability for maintaining those skill sets in the most cost-efficient way.

- In the New Normal, performers must be able to, at any moment, learn a new skill and integrate it into their existing skill framework. Often there isn't sufficient time to wait for a course to be developed and offered. They need to learn right now because they need to perform right now. This blend of formal and informal learner-performer support provides this capacity to immediately learn in response to changes in the business landscape.

- Few performers can learn and recall all the knowledge and skills they need to do their work. Most learners readily forget most of what they learn anyway. And what little amount learners do remember generally has such a short shelf-life that the capacity and disposition to unlearn is a fundamental learning requirement. Again, intentional Performance Support integrated with formal learning solves this challenge.

- At the moment of Apply, performers often need support in adapting what they know to meet the unique challenges at that moment and in some cases to learn more. In the real world, things also fail to work the way they should. The New Blend anticipates and meets these challenges.

These can be life-sustaining benefits to organizations today. Years ago one of us helped conduct an efficiency evaluation of a call center with 1,000 employees for what was then a major software company. We identified 200 questions that accounted for 80 percent of the calls hitting the center. Half the calls related to training issues. In discussion with the executive vice president who had responsibility for the center, we recommended a Performance Support solution integrated into the company's training offering. This could have cut the number of calls in half. His response proved tragic for the company: "That only accounts for a small percentage of our revenue," he said. "We have more important issues." The company doesn't exist today. Obviously there were other factors in play that destroyed it, but failing to adequately support its customers in their effort to successfully use the products the company produced was a primary factor.

Today, no organization can risk failure by ignoring wasted effort. In an environment of change, the time to performance is critical. This New Blend addresses the entire learning life cycle of performers where they are called upon to continuously learn, unlearn, relearn, and adapt.

Our effort here is to make the case for this New Blend. One of the challenges you will face as you work to articulate the need for blending formal with intentional informal learning is that these terms are understood by the learning industry but aren't as readily embraced by decision leaders outside the profession. We have found it helpful to couch these concepts in other terms.

When organizations establish Performance Support practices to intentionally support informal learning and then blend this into their formal learning practices in the ways described above, they have the makings of a *complete learning ecosystem.*

Learning ecosystems can exist at all levels in an organization (for example, work group, division, or company). A complete learning ecosystem provides performers, at any of those levels, the support they need to learn formally and informally. It consists of a common set of practices that provides people everything they need to learn something for the first time or learn more about it. These same practices also provide intuitive, tailored aid to those same people when they are called upon to apply what they learned, when things change or break. The success of any learning ecosystem is in its capacity to ensure and sustain the most effective performance always.

HOW YOU CAN APPLY THIS: DELIVER STRATEGIC VALUE AND EARN A SEAT AT THE TABLE

Here's the question: To what degree does the training function in your organization help set its business strategy, and then help drive it? Or is your training team so enwrapped in its own world of learning that it fails to engage beyond training issues contributing directly to the health and well-being of the organization it serves?

Here's what we need to do to move out from under overhead status and deliver obvious strategic value:

- Become students of leadership and business, as well as learning.
- Monitor the competitive landscape and the larger world.
- Develop ownership of strategy.
- Drive from those needs to the performance solutions we build and implement.

Becoming Students of Leadership and Business as well as Learning

The training function should be the proving ground for the top leaders in any organization. Today's New Normal calls for leaders who are dynamic learners, who can learn at or above the speed of change, who can lift those they lead to the same kind of learning patterns, and who can put in place organizational systems that optimize the learning agility of the organization as a whole. Leaders simply can't accomplish this without cultivating their capacity to *inspire, instruct,* and *apply* the fundamental principles that lead to business success.

How can individuals who desire to influence the well-being of a business through learning expect to do so if they lack the capacity to lead, fail to understand how leaders think, feel, and act, and fail to fully comprehend what makes a business successful?

In this New Normal, people who belong to the profession of teaching, training, and learning must extend their professional efforts beyond the technologies and practices of learning and instruction to embrace the fundamental principles of leadership, strategy, and business. Only then can the training arm sit down at the leadership table and legitimately contribute.

Monitoring the Competitive Landscape and the Larger World

As mentioned earlier, organizations today will flourish in the New Normal only to the degree they are able to learn at or above the speed of change. This kind of marketplace agility can be achieved and maintained only if the organization has in place the capacity to see change before it is upon them. According to Dr. Timothy R. Clark (see his commentary at the end of this chapter), organizations need to have in place a "distant early warning system" that identifies and tracks adaptive challenges coming their way. This intelligence function keeps the strategy function responsive to changes in the market landscape. Training needs to be a primary player in both of these arenas. Only then will it have the capacity to rapidly build and deploy the training and Performance Support system necessary for the organization to successfully respond ahead of those adaptive challenges.

Developing an Ownership of Strategy

Training's quest for strategic legitimacy must include engaging directly in the formulation, execution, and evolution of the strategic imperatives that drive the organization. A seat in the strategy room will never be gained by pounding on the door and demanding to be let in. The right to enter must be earned. The good news for training groups is that the nature of the New Normal presents a singular opportunity to do this. Those in training are best equipped to assist the organization in gathering and monitoring intelligence on potential market disrupters. This intelligence function necessarily informs the strategy function, which in turn informs the learning function so that it can put in place the requisite Performance Support solutions needed for the organization to learn at or above the speed of market change.

This is a far cry from where most organizations are today. It has never been enough to just align the corporate curriculum with business strategy. When the focus is solely on alignment, the training

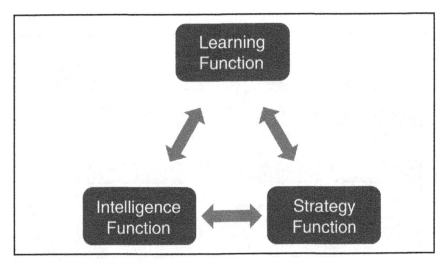

Figure 1.3. The TRCLARK Learning 3.0 Strategic Alignment Model
Source: Dr. Timothy R. Clark.

group remains in a reactive role. They are merely taking a strategy fed to them by those who are driving the business. This complacency falls way short of optimal. If we're truly interested in contributing strategically, we must earn the right to participate.

Driving from Strategy to the Training and PS Solutions We Build and Implement

The worst thing the training function can ever do is buy or build without first aligning it all with the strategic imperatives of the organization. Few ever admit to this, but the practices of alignment are often so superficial that they fail to truly drive alignment ahead of develop and buy. Obviously, even when they achieve alignment, because of the New Normal's unrelenting environment of change, there must be constant recalibrating to ensure that what is in place is contributing to its full potential. The bottom line is that strategy should drive the development and implementation of everything we do.

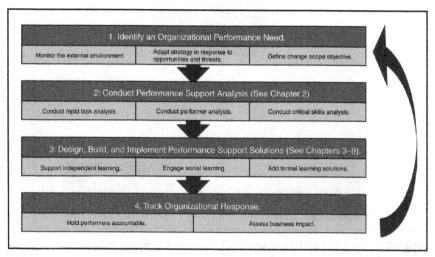

Figure 1.4. A Process Flow to Illustrate How Training Groups Can Deliver Strategic Value

The following list is a process flow that shows how training groups can deliver strategic value. The process flow is also shown in Figure 1.4.

1. **Identify an organizational performance need.** Here, as Clark suggests, strategic alignment is driven from the intelligence and strategy functions into the training function, not the other way around. This is a proactive approach. Through systematic information gathering and monitoring of the external environment, strategy is informed of potential threats and/or opportunities. The strategy function determines if the organization is adequately prepared to respond to these threats and/or opportunities. If it is not, organizational performance needs are identified and delivered to the training function in the form of a change scope objective to translate the need into the individual and collective performance requirements of its people. (Note: The strategy function also passes these needs to other parts of the organization to address adaption requirements in technology, product lines, communication, and so on.)

2. **Conduct PS analysis.** During this phase, the learning function identifies, by conducting a *rapid task analysis* (RTA), the new processes, tasks, and concepts performers need to learn. The learning function then maps these performances to specific roles within the organization (by conducting *performer analysis*), and it then determines the learning investment the organization should make in supporting the specific tasks and concepts (by conducting a *critical skills analysis*). Once this phase is completed, the training function has a clear, justifiable plan for closing the performance gap. (Chapter 2 provides specific instructions for conducting these analyses.)

3. **Design, build, and implement PS solutions.** At this point, the learning function develops the core Performance Support solutions that address the moment of Apply and deploys them according to the time requirements set by the realities of the speed of the pending change. In tandem, the social learning infrastructure is engaged to facilitate collaborative learning

and support. Finally, as justified, formal learning solutions are completed and implemented. (Chapter 4 provides specific decision and design guidelines. The remaining chapters in this book address principles for building and implementing.)

4. **Track organizational response.** Finally, the learning function provides leaders ongoing accountability reports on the state of the organization's adaptation. In addition, it gathers data to determine business impact. If in this process, there emerges other change requirements not reflected in the initial change-scope-objective process, the learning function passes this information back to the strategy function who determines the organizational response.

The intent of the above process description is to illustrate how the strategy alignment should flow in organizations. Hopefully through it you can also catch a glimpse of the strategic role the learning functions can play as their organizations work at thriving and surviving in the New Normal.

INSIGHTS FROM A THOUGHT LEADER: Dr. Timothy R. Clark

Dr. Timothy R. Clark is founder and chairman of TRCLARK LLC, a consulting organization that specializes in leadership development, strategy, and organizational transformation.

He is considered a world authority on the subject of change leadership and large-scale organizational change. He is the author of the critically acclaimed book Epic Change: How to Lead Change in the Global Age *(Wiley/Jossey-Bass, 2008). He also recently authored* The Leadership Test: Will You Pass? *In 2009 he co-led, with Dr. Gottfredson, a yearlong benchmarking study of 10 major firms' best practices in developing organizational learning agility—the capacity for an organization to learn at or above the speed of change.*

Before founding his own firm, Dr. Clark was CEO of Novations SDC, a consulting firm based in Boston, Massachusetts.

He earned a doctorate in social science from Oxford University, where he was a Fulbright and British Research Scholar. As an undergraduate at Brigham Young University, where he completed a triple degree, he was named a first-team Academic All-American football player.

The Pursuit of Organizational Learning Agility

This is adapted by Dr. Clark from a research report produced
by TRCLARK titled: "In Search of Learning Agility"

The global age is here. With it comes a competitive environment unparalleled in intensity. Seasoned leaders used to claim they had seen most every problem several times before. That's no longer true. Today, organizations face a "New Normal." By definition, this New Normal is a highly dynamic environment where it's imperative to respond to continuous cycles of adaptive challenge and adaptive response.

The ultimate source of adaptive capacity, competitiveness, and self-preservation—indeed, the key to resilience and renewal—is inarguably continuous learning and knowledge application. This capability precedes and underlies much-discussed organizational capabilities like innovation, execution, and adaptive or preemptive response. As Mai Boliang, president of China's CIMC, the world's largest manufacturer of dry-cargo and refrigerated containers, aptly observes, "Our slogan is 'learn, improve, and disrupt.'"[4]

Of course the natural cycles of competitive advantage are nothing new. But if the half-life of an organization's knowledge mirrors its competitive strategy, organizations clearly face an accelerated learning requirement. The compression of time frames is shifting the source of ongoing competitiveness to learning as a core organizational competency. Unless an organization can learn at or above the speed of change in its environment, it faces the grave risk of irrelevance and failure.[5]

Organizations must undergo new learning cycles to prepare for new competitive cycles and accept that they need to constantly retool in order to maintain their edge. But most organizations struggle mightily to endure the buffetings of competitive pressure. However, this isn't a general plea for organizations simply to get learning. Unbounded and unprioritized learning can actually make things worse. Learning imperatives vary greatly among organizations; each organization has to prioritize its learning needs based on its strategic objectives. The point is that too few organizations learn fast enough or well enough.

Under normal market conditions, organizations don't compete beyond the bounds of their ability to learn. Creating an organization with *learning agility*—one that learns and responds quickly to adaptive challenge—may be the central organizational challenge of our time.[6] Edward J. Ludwig, chairman and CEO of medical technology firm Becton, Dickinson, affirms that "this is not new, but the emphasis, the urgency to deploy this kind of agile learning organization, is intensifying. The world is rapidly increasing its ability to throw the unexpected at you."[7]

Having a good strategy and being able to execute that strategy delivers competitiveness today. But sooner or later, the competitive advantage you enjoy today will come to an end. That's when an organization's learning agility is put to the test.

Defining Learning Agility

Learning agility refers to an organization's ability to respond to adaptive challenge—be it an opportunity, threat, or crisis—through the acquisition and application of knowledge and skills. High-agility organizations are able to learn quickly and apply effectively the collective knowledge and skills of their members, whereas low-agility organizations respond slowly and clumsily to adaptive challenge. At an organizational level, agility is the ability to grow, change, or innovate at or above the speed of one's own market. Anything less cannot be considered agility.

Let's make two important distinctions: First, agility is different from competence. *Competence* refers to an organization's ability to meet the challenges of today. It means that you have requisite knowledge and skills and that you are harvesting those assets through application and value creation. *Learning agility*, on the other hand, is the ability to continuously acquire new knowledge and skills assets during or ahead of changes in the market. An organization may be highly competent today, but competence today is not necessarily a good predictor of future competence: learning agility is. It provides the best-known gauge of future competitiveness. Some of the best organizations today will stumble and fail tomorrow precisely because they are not learning with or ahead of their markets.

A second distinction is that organizational learning agility is not simply the sum of the learning agility of its members. It's an organizational capacity that extends beyond the people in it. For example, Procter & Gamble's "Connect and Develop" process of external collaboration is a world-class agility asset through which it has engaged in over 1,000 external partnerships to generate innovations in technology, products, and services. The process, which is a combination of technology and organizational support processes, is both push and pull as it solicits solutions from the outside for identified needs as well as inviting new ideas for consideration. The program is a clear example of an agility asset that exists independent of individual employees.[8]

Required in the New Normal: Dynamic Learners and Leaders

No organization can survive in this New Normal if its learning mindset remains entrenched in the old ways of learning. Figure 1.5 shows the transformation all learners must make to remain competitive in today's environment of unrelenting change. The primary goal of the learning function in today's world should be to cultivate and support dynamic learners who are rapid,

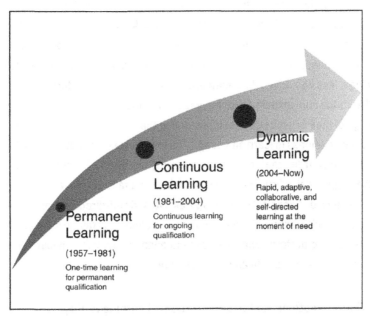

Figure 1.5. The Transformations All Learners Must Make
Source: Dr. Timothy R. Clark.

adaptive, collaborative, and self-directed in their approach to learning. This learning mindset is especially crucial for leaders at every level.

The new model of leadership for this New Normal requires a level of humility and curiosity that is simply alien to most traditional conceptions of leadership. Ironically, leaders are being challenged to develop confidence in the very act of not knowing. They now need to be able to acknowledge publicly when reality moves beyond their knowledge and skills and to trust in their own ability to learn and adapt. They must submit to the fact that they will pass through periods of temporary incompetence in their market and technical knowledge as they move through learning and change cycles. But if they can do this while retaining their underlying ability and willingness to learn, they will be able to stay in the game.

As MIT professor Edgar Schein has observed, for a leader to engage the entire organization in learning, "Leaders must learn something new. Before anyone else changes, leaders must overcome their own cultural assumptions and perceive new ways of doing things and new contexts in which to do them."[9] It has always been true that followers endow leaders with the credibility and legitimacy to lead. What's different in the New Normal is that credibility is based on personifying the qualities of a *high-performance learner*, rather than a traditional "expert."

Indeed, there is a new "learning leader" paradigm. It may in fact be the biggest shift in emphasis in leadership development theory in several decades. As a pattern, the learning leader is exceptionally attuned to the changing environment and the perishable nature of competitive advantage. Because of this ongoing acknowledgment, the learning leader is less wedded to trappings of status and privilege, less ego driven, less concerned with subordinate deference, and certainly less attached to the status quo. Instead, learning leaders are more concerned with understanding the changing ecology of their organizations and protecting the value the organization has created, through a vigilance and readiness to learn and adapt. The learning leader understands that learning is where advantage comes from, that it represents the highest form of enterprise risk management—and that the biggest risk a firm can take is to let learning falter. It seems increasingly clear that leaders who don't possess deep patterns of aggressive and self-directed learning in their dispositions are destined to fail, whereas the ones who do are almost certain to succeed—provided they combine those learning patterns with the ability to engage people.[10] The learning leader not only learns but is also always accessible and never remote.

Table 1.1: Five Factors That Promote or Hinder Organizational Learning Agility

1	**Intelligence function:** Observing market conditions, attractiveness, and opportunities for sustained profitability based on competitive position as well as monitoring the relative stability of the industry. It also includes monitoring opportunities and threats in the broader external landscape, including patterns, trends, shocks, and dislocations.
2	**Learning mindset:** The prevailing assumptions about how people learn, their dispositions toward learning, and that their learning habits and roles ought to be based on conventional thought and also immediate market forces within an industry. It is the paradigm of the period and yet also the willingness to challenge that paradigm.
3	**Leadership behavior:** The dominant themes and patterns of leadership during a particular time period.
4	**Organizational support:** Processes, systems, structures, and other forms of support that organizations provide to help employees in their coordinated learning and execution activities.
5	**Learning technology:** The common and emerging forms of technology that most organizations are using to enable learning.

Source: Dr. Timothy R. Clark

How Ready Is Your Organization to Learn at or above the Speed of Change?

In September 2008, TRCLARK issued a research report titled "In Search of Learning Agility." In this research, five primary factors, as listed in Table 1.1, surfaced as having a critical impact on the promotion or hindrance of organizational learning agility across the broad spectrum.

No organization can attain and sustain learning agility without attending to these five factors and pursuing best practices in each of these areas.

Factor 1. The Intelligence Function

With the speed, complexity, and unpredictability of this global age comes unprecedented political and economic interdependency. What happens in Vegas doesn't stay in Vegas. A disruption in a different market in a far-off place can deliver a crippling blow to unsuspecting companies that have chosen to simply "mind their own business." Table 1.2 lists some questions for you to answer regarding your organization's agility level in this area.

Factor 2. The Learning Mindset

Clearly, learning agility has, at its core, learners who are agile in how they learn. They are rapid, adaptive, collaborative, and self-directed in how they learn. This *dynamic learning mindset* must be developed and supported by organizations pursuing agility. If an organization's workforce is caught in outdated mindsets, organizational learning agility will continue to be a nice topic to discuss, but it won't see the light of day in real-world application.

One of the key areas of best practices for cultivating this dynamic learning mindset is in guiding employees in social networking. Members of Generation Y (the "millennials") are adept learners with social networking tools and other digital media. They are also, for the most part, self-taught and deeply socialized learners in this domain. They are digital natives, having grown up with these tools. This leaves a demographic and cultural divide in most organizations that separates the baby boomers in a fairly pronounced way from millennials, with Generation Xers somewhere in the middle. The challenge is that most baby boomers cannot close the learning gap on their own. They need guidance and training in the process.

Finally, the employee population demonstrates a general need even across demographic cohorts for guidance in the use of social networking and digital media as learning tools. Employees are prone to fall into patterns of inefficiency and ineffectiveness. Most need help in developing skills to know when these tools are helpful and in avoiding supersaturation, working memory overload, nonproductive learning, or irrelevant learning. Organizations should consider more carefully the *return on instruction* for teaching employees how to develop skills

Table 1.2: Factor 1. The Intelligence Function

Questions	1 Not at All	2	3 Partway There	4	5 Mostly There	6	7 In Place and Functioning Effectively
1 To what degree has my organization established a comprehensive, balanced, and systematic process for gathering, integrating, and interpreting intelligence from different domains that might bear on the competitive position of the organization?							
2 To what degree have we established the framework or logic to help organize, prioritize, and inform the organization of the information it is gathering?							
3 To what degree is the learning function engaged in this intelligence gathering and analysis?							

Source: Dr. Timothy R. Clark

for problem definition, scoping, searching, filtering, integrating, and interpreting to replace the haphazard, ad hoc, free-flow, and stream-of-consciousness patterns of learning that so many employees demonstrate. It may be time for learning organizations to take a step back and offer new "learn-how-to-learn" solutions to help employees learn in the digital environment. Even the digital natives, who are natural swimmers in social networking and digital media, don't necessarily know how to learn in the domain. Table 1.3 lists some questions for you to answer regarding your organization's agility level in this area.

Table 1.3: Factor 2. The Learning Mindset

	Questions	1 Not at All	2	3 Partway There	4	5 Mostly There	6	7 In Place and Functioning Effectively
4	To what degree is my organization intentionally developing dynamic learners who are rapid, adaptive, collaborative, and self-directed?							
5	To what degree does my organization intentionally support informal learning via Performance Support, social learning, and so on?							
6	To what degree are learners receiving training, during their formal learning events, to use Performance Support tools and social learning media?							

Source: Dr. Timothy R. Clark

Factor 3. The Leadership Behavior

The leadership behavior change required to take organizations to "continuous, rapid, and collaborative learning at the moment of need" is significant. It shifts the definition of competence from knowledge and skills to the ability to acquire knowledge and skills. Competence is now a matter of individual learning agility. Not surprisingly, this definition is personally threatening at worst and psychologically unsafe at best for many leaders today. Yet leaders must stand first in line to model the habits and patterns of a high-performance learner. This not only requires a fundamental change from the leader-as-expert model but it also requires leaders to assume a very different emotional and social posture. Leaders must become comfortable portraying themselves as competent by virtue of their ability to learn and adapt rather than on the basis of their current knowledge and skills.

Indeed, we are starting to see the emergence of a new "dynamic learning leader" paradigm. It may in fact be the biggest shift in emphasis in leadership development theory in several decades. As a pattern, the dynamic learning leader is exceptionally attuned to the changing environment and the perishable nature of competitive advantage. Because of this ongoing acknowledgment, the dynamic learning leader is less wedded to trappings of status and privilege, less ego driven, less yearning for deference, and certainly less attached to the status quo. Instead, dynamic learning leaders are more concerned with understanding the changing ecology of their organizations and protecting the value the organization has created through a vigilance and readiness to learn and adapt. The dynamic learning leader understands that learning is where advantage comes from, that it represents the highest form of enterprise risk management, and that the biggest risk a firm can take is to cease to learn. Table 1.4 lists some questions for you to answer regarding your organization's agility level in this area.

Factor 4. The Organizational Support

High-agility organizations support learners at all of the following Five Moments of Learning Need:

1. Learning how to do something *New* for the first time
2. Learning *More* based on prior learning experience
3. Learning at the moment when learners *Apply* what they have learned as they do their actual work
4. Learning when things go wrong in order to *Solve* a problem
5. Learning when things *Change* in order to adapt to new ways of doing things

As a simple diagnostic, an organization can measure its fundamental learning agility by assessing its capacity to address these Five Moments of Learning Need. As organizations put in place systems that facilitate learning agility, those systems must be aligned and integrated in an efficient and intuitive way to accommodate performance during every one of them.

There are other critical aspects of organizational support. Learning agility is a co-creative process that springs from richly enabled interactions within and beyond the organization. There must be a process-oriented view of the business as a whole rather than as fragmented sets of siloed activities.

Table 1.4: Factor 3. The Leadership Behavior

Questions		1 Not at All	2	3 Part-way There	4	5 Mostly There	6	7 In Place and Func-tioning Effec-tively
7	How prepared is my organization for the transition from the leader-as-expert paradigm to one that emphasizes the leader-as learner?							
8	To what extent is the personal credibility of leaders in my organization based on their personal learning agility as opposed to old knowledge?							
9	How much do the leaders in my organization lean on the machinery of the organization to govern their personal learning path?							
10	How effective are the leaders in my organization at calling forth the discretionary efforts and creative potential of other people through the influence of their learning habits, curiosity, and enthusiasm in the face of problems that don't yet have answers?							
11	To what extent can the leaders in my organization engage and mobilize people based on their influence skills rather than hiding behind the artifacts of title, position, and authority to press people into service?							
12	To what degree do the leaders in my organization feel personally threatened by the fact that their knowledge and skills are becoming obsolete?							

(continued)

13	To what degree are the leaders in my organization psychologically prepared to show their vulnerability to incompetence as their skills become outdated because they have the ability to learn and adapt?							
14	To what degree do the leaders in my organization believe that learning is where advantage comes from, that it represents the highest form of enterprise risk management, and that the biggest risk a firm can take is to cease to learn?							

Source: Dr. Timothy R. Clark

In addition, highly agile organizations embrace collaborative learning and apply effectively the collective knowledge and skills within and even beyond their borders. Collective knowledge and skills encompass not only what is resident and evolving within people but also all that has been captured and stored along the way, made and kept useful in a form that is immediately accessible and adaptive to individual needs. Table 1.5 lists some questions for you to answer regarding your organization's agility level in this area.

Factor 5. The Learning Technology

Technology is an elixir that can intoxicate the best of learning leaders. It has certainly enticed many into technical binges that yielded nothing more than a long hangover. As organizations step into a full-out pursuit of learning agility, they must guard against being techno-dazzled by pursuing technology only as a means for enabling the previous four factors. With this caution, here is some promising news:

The learning technology market is finally turning serious attention to the informal side of learning. In response, Performance Support, authoring, delivery, and brokering tools are entering the marketplace. In addition, performer-generated content through social networking is extending Performance Support capacity in response to the widespread need for fingertip knowledge support.

Learning Content Management (LCM) is also reasserting itself in the form of multichannel publishing from single-sourced, metadata-enriched content. Other broader knowledge management

Table 1.5: Factor 4. The Organizational Support

	Questions	1 Not at All	2	3 Part-way There	4	5 Mostly There	6	7 In Place and Func-tioning Effectively
15	To what degree has my organization addressed all Five Moments of Learning Need?							
16	To what degree is there a process-oriented view of the business as a whole rather than as fragmented sets of siloed activities?							
17	To what degree does my organization support collaborative learning and apply effectively the collective knowledge and skills within and even beyond its borders?							

Source: Dr. Timothy R. Clark

technologies and practices are beginning to wrap around these LCM systems, enhancing the ability to capture, store, manage, and maximize the usefulness of content capital.

Other types of technology that accelerate collaborative work are integrating as mashups, further disallowing structure, aggregating human capability, and harnessing innovation and value out of what, at a tactical level, is a chaotic creative process.

And as Web 2.0 tools and systems continue to integrate, orchestrate, and extend across the traditional siloed boundaries within and beyond the formal structures and firewalls of organizations, they will continue to enhance but not drive learning agility.

All of this reflects a beginning of what technology can and is doing to help organizations learn at or above the speed of change. The key, here, is to apply these technologies to this vital mission. Table 1.6 lists some questions for you to answer regarding your organization's agility level in this area.

Moving Forward with Initiatives That Cultivate Organizational Learning Agility

Here are some initiatives that merit your best efforts to bring them to fruition. No other part of your organization is in a better position to operationalize these initiatives. And, if you don't

Table 1.6: Factor 5. The Learning Technology

	Questions	1 Not at All	2	3 Partway There	4	5 Mostly There	6	7 In Place and Functioning Effectively
18	To what degree is technology strengthening the effectiveness of formal learning?							
19	To what degree is technology supporting performance during the informal side of learning?							
20	To what degree is technology enabling learning agility across my organization?							

Source: Dr. Timothy R. Clark

take them on, someone else will. Don't abdicate this opportunity to lead out in your organization's pursuit of learning agility.

1. **Unify learning and other support functions to cultivate learning agility.** Performance Support can serve as a common catalyst for unifying and aligning the efforts of training and other Performance Support groups such as help desks and technical publications. These groups have been fragmented long enough. Maximum learning agility requires these silos to disappear. This doesn't require any real organizational boundary changes. It simply requires the establishment of common practices under a common charter. That charter needs

to be driven by a commitment to delivering strategic value by cultivating learning agility. Ultimately, if what these groups do doesn't unitedly contribute to people's ability to grow, respond, change, and innovate at or above the speed of the market, they will fail their companies.

2. **Integrate learning and Performance Support practices to address formal and informal learning at all Five Moments of Learning Need.** The widespread recognition that most learning is informal is turning attention to developing Performance Support capabilities for informal learning. But the solutions identified must be implemented with formal learning still in mind. It is in the formal learning environment that self-directed learning and self-support are either initiated and reinforced or undermined. Self-directed learning, self-support, and learning collaboration must become primary instructional objectives in formal training. Employees should be trained to use Performance Support solutions that will be available to them when they're "on their own." Many need to learn how to become independent learners for the first time in their lives, using those tools. They also need to learn how to collaborate in problem-solving and ad hoc learning situations when necessary.

3. **Cultivate evaluation as an individual and organizational competency.** High-agility organizations today are different from those that are not based on their evaluation capacity. They cultivate it as an individual and organizational core competency. Evaluation is the analysis and interpretation of performance. It is the study of relationships and causation. It is also the dispassionate and nonpoliticized consideration of contribution. Most individuals and organizations are profoundly poor at evaluation precisely because they were acculturated under a learning tradition and mindset that emphasized "one-time learning for permanent qualification." This mindset has conditioned individuals to evaluate both people and situations based on a slow-moving industrial context. As a consequence, many employees are dependent learners with old tools, old frameworks, and old criteria. Further, many employees are highly unskilled in their ability to evaluate themselves and their peers. Yet these skills are vital when individuals and organizations are confronted with turbulent change. Evaluation capacity is a necessary precondition to learning agility; it is the taproot of adaptive response and innovation.

4. **Cultivate an organizational culture and leadership behavior that supports learning agility.** Culture is about patterns. It's about what most people in an organization think and do most of the time. Whenever people come together to form a collective, a culture is born not immediately, but gradually. It's the natural result of social forces exerted through everyday interaction. With time, patterns of thinking and behavior develop and calcify within the organization.

When any organization begins the pursuit of agility, culture will inevitably get in the way. For this reason, leaders need to identify cultural liabilities and work to turn them into cultural assets. Through deliberate means, organizations have the opportunity to design and cultivate the culture they need rather than live with culture that blocks learning agility.

Culture change is a matter of finding the points of leverage that shape culture in the first place. Fortunately, those levers are the same regardless of the nature, composition, and purpose of the organization. There are of course differences based on industry and market, but the same basic set of levers shapes culture in every context. The most important levers of culture have to do with what is

- Modeled
- Communicated
- Taught
- Measured
- Recognized
- Rewarded

Of all of the levers that shape organizational culture, the single most important one is the factor of leadership behavior. Leaders shape culture through "modeling" or demonstrating behavior. Organizational cultures don't change unless leadership behavior is manifestly different and reflects the desired culture. But there is a caveat: Of all the categories of organizational change, changing culture is the most difficult because it is rooted in human behavior. You should expect a culture change effort to take longer and require more effort than other types of organizational change, such as changes to structure, process, systems, technology, capital assets, or cost cutting. Culture tends to preserve and protect itself against change. Over time, culture becomes hard and encrusted as thought and behavioral patterns become entrenched.

5. **Continuously grow and manage unrestrained content capital.** Content becomes capital when it's captured and made useful to the organization. Content becomes unrestrained when it's free from proprietary formats or delivery forms. Learning agility requires that organizations continually capture content and make it available in many different forms that are tailored to the individual and role requirements of different people. And it all needs to be up-to-date. All of these content management requirements can be met with current technologies such as multichannel publishing and user-generated content. Yet the movement toward content capital management has been slow because organizations have seldom been able to make the business case for the investment. What's changing this is the growing number

of organizations that have been caught flat-footed when their markets were besieged with new entrants, disruptive technologies, or other unforeseen threats.

A growing number of organizations are able to cost-justify content capital management on the basis of *multichannel publishing* alone. This is where content is developed and stored as a single source and then transformed into other forms at any time. For example, a single-sourced procedure could be transformed into an online help file, a Web-based learning course, an online reference job aid, and a pdf, case-based practice guide. And since the content isn't locked into any proprietary format, the case-based practice guide could also be published as a Word file in addition to the pdf file. This same procedure can also be pushed as data into a virtual lab where the lab scenarios would automatically incorporate the procedure into a practice scenario.

Contrary to popular thought, the challenge of content asset management is not with the technology; it is with the practices associated with how content has historically been created, managed, and produced into its various forms. Within most organizations there is significant duplication of effort. The elimination of that duplication, alone, often justifies the investment. There are significant efficiencies that can be brought to bear as well. A second, less quantifiable benefit is the ability to capture performer-generated content, which is becoming a crucial component of successful strategy execution.

6. **Drive collaboration within and beyond the organization.** When organizations begin addressing the formal and informal learning needs of people, the strategic value of collaborative learning becomes clear. Ad hoc collaboration within and beyond the organization is crucial to organizational agility. Historically, this collaboration was limited to those within earshot of the individual employee. This so-called sneakernet support where peers helped one another based on geographic proximity has been shallow, random, and costly. Collaboration tools have dramatically changed the rules of the game. But the adoption of new collaborative technologies has been slow across the board. The primary reasons are limited demand and ineffective implementation. Organizations simply haven't found the value proposition to engage most employees.

Part of the solution is to make collaboration readily accessible, intuitive, and helpful. Helpfulness is determined by an upfront assessment of collaboration needs at every level of the organization. The technology solution should be fitted to meet those exact needs. Virtual communities can become an effective way to drive collaboration within and beyond the organization. Certainly, Generation X and, to a greater extent, Generation Y have been weaned on these types of collaborative environments. But much of the current workforce is unfamiliar and uncomfortable with new forms of collaboration. Leaders have to be willing to make a significant training investment to help them adopt these new technologies.

7. **Push ownership of learning to the front line and to the learners themselves.** Front-line supervisors have the ability to see the immediate cause and effect of learning in the workplace. They witness the application of new knowledge and skills and see the consequences. Not surprisingly, when front-line managers believe that certain learning solutions will help their people be more successful in their work, they commit themselves to provide those solutions wherever possible. Because of this personal commitment and the unique line-of-sight vantage point of the front-line manager, learning outcomes are usually stronger when managed at this level. A second point is that when employees are committed and independent learners, learning outcomes increase again.

A Singular Opportunity

Two decades ago, Peter Senge challenged organizations to become learning organizations. He argued that organizations must be able to adapt quickly and effectively if they wished to excel in their field or market. His work initially received widespread lip service, but most organizations ignored him when it came to their day-to-day practices. Why? Because the markets, at that time, didn't demand agility, and the framework he proposed didn't consider all the factors that govern agility. Today, when agility is no less than the entrance fee for survival, the five factors presented above provide an actionable framework for pursuing it.

2

SUPPORTING PERFORMANCE @ ALL FIVE MOMENTS OF NEED

One must learn by doing the thing; for though you think you
know it, you have no certainty, until you try.

—*Sophocles*

A STORY TO GET STARTED: CON'S FIRST KISS

My sister taught me how to kiss—she didn't train me. Had she
done so, we couldn't use this story to start this chapter. She gave
me some wonderful pointers, but the night I made my first attempt
to move from simply understanding to actual application, I learned
a vital lesson. My friend Paul Teichert had warned me that if I didn't
kiss Connie Black soon, she was going to start to date Shane McQuen.
Well, after my first attempt, even with all my sister had taught me, Connie started dating Shane. The quote from Sophocles at the beginning
of this chapter describes best the lesson I learned. Though I thought I
knew how to go about it, I had no certainty until I actually acted upon
what I had learned. And at that moment, I gained absolute certainty
that I didn't know enough to perform successfully.

Behind this lesson is the reality that there are actually Five Moments
of Learning Need. My first kiss covered only two of those moments. If
your learning strategy doesn't embrace all five, you'll run short when it
comes to effective performance. Sustained successful performance re-

quires a broader view than the learning industry has generally taken.

This broader view includes realities beyond those I faced with my first kiss. Today, few people, if any, work in complete isolation. The mastery of a single skill or even a set of skills is only an initial step to competency. Real performance most often requires the integration of personal and collective skill sets in a collaborative work environment that is in a state of constant flux. In this environment any approach to learning has to consider factors such as these:

- Learners must learn how to perform effectively, together, in a state of interdependence within and beyond their specific work groups.
- Because most learners work in an environment where their skill sets are in a state of continual flux, there must be an intentional plan in place for maintaining those skill sets.
- Learners must be able to, at any moment, learn a new skill and integrate it into their existing skill framework. This may happen when there isn't sufficient time to wait for a course to be developed and offered.
- Few performers can learn all the knowledge and skills they need to do their work. Most learners readily forget most of what they learn. And what little amount learners do remember generally has such a short shelf-life that the capacity and disposition to unlearn is a fundamental learning requirement.
- At the moment of Apply, performers often need support in adapting what they know to meet the unique challenges at that moment and in some cases learn more.
- The real world of performance requires support when things fail to work the way they should.

This chapter discusses the Five Moments of Learning Need that address the above factors. They encompass the complete journey of gaining and maintaining competency.

Read on if you want to learn how to accomplish this by supporting performance at all Five Moments of Learning Need.

THE FIVE MOMENTS OF LEARNING NEED

By way of review:

> A *complete learning ecosystem* comprises all the factors that support a vibrant learning community of interdependent people in gaining and maintaining the skills necessary to perform effectively together. It can exist at different scales in an organization (for example, a work group, division, or company).

In order for a learning ecosystem to be complete, it must support the entire journey performers make from the beginning stages of learning through the full range of challenges that can occur at the moment of Apply—when they are called upon to actually perform. There are five fundamental moments that make up the full range of Performance Support needs people have in their journey of becoming and remaining competent in their individual and collective work.

The training industry has focused its practices primarily upon the first two moments of need:

1. **New:** When people are learning how to do something for the first time
2. **More:** When people are expanding the breadth and depth of what they have learned

Documentation teams have historically assumed primary responsibility for providing printed and online help information for people to use when they face the third moment of need:

3. **Apply:** When they need to act on what they have learned, which includes planning what they will do, remembering what they may have forgotten, or adapting their performance to a unique situation

Help desk practices have also assumed a role in supporting people in this third area of need. But their primary work has been to address the fourth moment:

4. **Solve:** When problems arise, or things break or don't work the way they were intended

Finally, there is a moment of need that few organizations have addressed well:

5. **Change:** When people need to learn a new way of doing something that requires them to change skills that are deeply ingrained in their performance practices

We've had the opportunity to view up close the efforts of hundreds of organizations in addressing these Five Moments of Learning Need. In almost every case their combined efforts have been limited, fragmented, and wasteful. Now this is not to say that great work isn't going on in each of these Performance Support silos, but the people we are charged to train and support deserve "intuitive, tailored aid" that is orchestrated together to "ensure the most effective personal and collective performance" during all five moments of need. Solving this requires an understanding of the role of performer support during each of these five moments of need.

What Is the Role of Performance Support during the First Two Moments of Need?

The primary benefits of Performance Support are achieved during the final three moments of need (applying, solving, and changing). But a common challenge in these areas is whether or not people choose to use the "tailored aid" available to them. Often this aid isn't as intuitive as it should be. Also, some performers aren't as independent as they need to be to cause them to take full advantage of the Performance Support offerings.

It is during the (1) start-up and (2) ongoing moments of learning need that performers can learn how to use the Performance Support aids you are making available to them. It is also vital that you help performers become more self-reliant in their disposition to using these aids.

In addition, Performance Support aids can change the scope and nature of formal learning events. For example, when you have an embedded job aid that will walk a person through software-related tasks as they actually perform those tasks, then why not teach performers how to use that job aid and then focus their learning on the skills that are more critical to business processes and collaborative work?

What Is the Role of Performance Support at the Moment of Apply?

This is the sweet spot of Performance Support. There is much that can and needs to occur here. And today we can do more than we have been able to do in the past. When people are at this moment, when they need to actually perform on the job, they need instant access to tools that will intuitively help them do just that: perform. This help must be immediate and tailored to the role and situation of the performer. The aid needs to allow the performer to dive as deeply as necessary to plan, remember, adapt, or reference information required for successful performance.

What Is the Role of Performance Support at the Moment of Solve?

In the real world, things don't always work as intended. When this happens, performers are pushed to troubleshoot and resolve those problems. This is another area where Performance Support practices deliver great value. Often the job aids created for this moment of need are tools that walk performers through the problem-solving process—automating all that is possible to automate.

What Is the Role of Performance Support
at the Moment of Change?

This moment of need has been the least attended to and yet it is the most challenging. And since we don't attend to it very well, it is often the most costly to organizations. Once skills have become ingrained into the work practices of people and organizations, replacing those out-of-date practices with new ways of performing is a significant learning challenge. This need cannot be adequately met by only bringing performers into formal learning events devoted to teaching "the new ways" of doing things. Rather, these performers absolutely need job aids that will guide them through the new way each time they are called upon by their job to perform. This challenge is ultimately resolved over time on the job.

THE CHALLENGES OF APPLY

Although the first two moments of need (learn New and learn More) are initially satisfied by the development and delivery of formal learning events, these two can also occur at the moment of Apply. It is highly probable, in today's work environment, that a performer may need to learn something New for the first time or learn More right at the moment of Apply—when there simply isn't time to step away from the workflow and take a traditional course. Performers need to learn it in real time while on the job at the moment of Apply.

The moments of Change and Solve also occur at the moment of Apply, but they present unique challenges that distinguish them from traditional Apply challenges. They'll be addressed in greater detail later in this chapter. All four of these moments, though, are or can be nested in the moment of Apply.

The bottom line? Organizations need in place a performer support strategy that accommodates all of these moments of need at the moment of Apply—while people are "doing" their job.

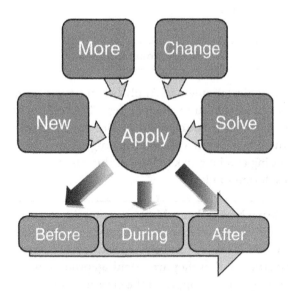

Figure 2.1. How the Moments of Need Relate to the Moment of Apply

But this is not all. The strategy must also address the three time phases of Apply: the time before performance, the time during performance, and the time after performance ends.

Figure 2.1 shows how the moments of need can be nested into the moment of Apply. It also shows the three phases of Apply impacting this critical moment of Apply. The elephant in this room is the need for organizations to address the challenges performers face at each of these moments during all three phases. Chapter 4 discusses how you can address all of these.

Table 2.1 lists some of the challenges that the elephant can cause. If you want to know how your organization is doing in the area of performer support, read through each of these challenges and ask yourself these two questions:

1. How critical is it that our organization address this challenge?
2. How effectively is our organization at meeting this challenge?

Table 2.1. The Challenges at the Moment of Apply

Challenge	Additional Comments
1. Performers may have forgotten what they learned during formal learning events.	This is the typical moment of Apply (when people forget). There is high probability that this is happening. The shelf life of most formal training outcomes is hours, not days. But the good news is that once something is learned in a formal learning setting, the journey to remembering can be quick as long as there is an effective performer support solution in place.
2. They may not have learned what they needed to learn in their formal learning courses in the first place.	This is a learn New or learn More situation. Most learners mentally check in and out throughout a training event. Too often the lights are on, but nobody's home. Just because learners are present in a class doesn't guarantee that they are listening, processing, and expending the effort to grasp and apply all the class intends to teach. Often when people are in the actual trenches of Apply, the need to learn becomes compellingly clear. At this moment there may not be sufficient time for the performer to move through a complete e-learning course inside an LMS. Short, potent learning bursts can be more impactful here.
3. Performers might not know enough, requiring them to learn More right at the moment of Apply.	Although performers may have mastered the objectives of a formal training class, sometimes the objectives don't cover everything that the real world dishes out. In addition, today's work calls for competency levels that would challenge any performer to master it all and any organization to provide the training resources to facilitate that mastery via the traditional classroom.
4. At the moment of Apply, circumstances may be so different from what performers were trained to address that they may need help adapting.	Developing generalizable skills requires the use of instructional methods during formal learning events that are paired with intuitive access to rich content stores and culturally sustained social media resources at the moment of Apply.
5. Tools, systems, technologies, and equipment don't work the way they are supposed to work.	Developing diagnostic or problem-solving skills requires the use of instructional methods during formal learning events that are paired with intuitive access to rich content stores and culturally sustained social media resources at the moment of Apply.

6. Performers must change to a new way of performing.	Today's New Normal environment of change requires transient skill-set development through which performers continuously unlearn so that they can relearn new ways of performing. This is an ever-present challenge in the New Normal.
7. Performers need to continuously improve their performance.	Objective self-appraisal immediately following performance requires access to unobtrusive, highly portable self-assessment tools as part of an organization's performer support strategy.
8. PS solutions must support integrated, collaborative skill sets before, during, and after the moment of Apply.	It isn't enough to provide performers with job aides in support of independent mastery of singular skills. Competency is much more complex, requiring the brokering of a full range of learning assets in support of integrated collaborative skill sets across the Five Moments of Learning Need, when it is needed in the form it's needed.

THERE'S NO TOUGHER CHALLENGE THAN CHANGE

Change impacts how we address the moment of Apply. Change is a fundamental reality in today's work environment. It is often unpredictable, absolutely unrelenting, and, more often than not, terribly unforgiving. Alvin Toffler, writer and futurist, has observed that change, today, is "nonlinear and can go backwards, forwards, and sideways." In his book *Rethinking the Future,* he further describes how we must respond to this dynamic change environment:

The illiterate of the twenty-first century will not be those who cannot read and write, but those who cannot learn, unlearn, and relearn.

The fundamental difference between how we support performers at the moment of Change and how we do so at the typical moment of Apply lies in the requirement change makes of performers to "unlearn" and then "relearn" a new way. Our profession, for the most part, hasn't provided the support it can and should when performers face this performance twist. Here are a couple of recommendations:

Take on the Challenge of Deep-Rooted Change

Years ago, after one of us completed working for a client, a participant in the project offered to provide a ride to the airport to allow continued discussion. After a long drive, seeing no planes in the air anywhere, the question was asked, "How long before we arrive at the airport?" As the driver hit his breaks, he turned and said, "I'm almost home." Has something like this ever happened to you—where you have acted in an automated way?

The cognitive principle at play in such circumstances is *automaticity*. Things that we do, over and over, tend to become automated in our skill set—to the point that we can do them without conscious thought. And when this has occurred within a workforce and the workforce is then called upon to change that automated performance, organizations face one of the most significant performer support challenges it can face.

Software companies have paid dearly in their failure to provide meaningful solutions to this moment of Change—when skills have become deep rooted. For example, it is not uncommon to see software vendors force feed newly released software upgrades through their market channels. There is often very little pull from the marketplace. Why? Because with all the hyped capabilities, the software too often lacks the Performance Support infrastructure necessary to help people unlearn their automated skills and relearn how to perform the same tasks within the new software. If these venders would actually provide this support, not only would the uptake by their existing customer base be dramatically faster (thereby accelerating revenues) but the goodwill generated within that customer base would suppress competing market forces.

When organizations face any major change initiative, there is high probability that there are deep-rooted skills that require overriding. This can best be done with a robust solution that supports performers in their workflow, at the moment of Apply when they are called upon to unlearn and relearn. Too few change initiatives adequately make this crucial investment.

This challenge of deep-rooted change has been around for a long time. We now have the knowledge and wherewithal to address it directly. We simply need to understand the realities of deep-rooted change and step up to it, ahead of it, before it's upon us.

Grow Dynamic Learners

As mentioned in the previous chapter, there is a new era of change confronting organizations today. This unpredictable, unrelenting, and unforgiving environment of change requires organizations to cultivate dynamic learners—learners who know how to be rapid, adaptive, and collaborative in how they learn, unlearn, and relearn. Today's learners must cultivate a mindset that anticipates change. These dynamic performers must also have access to tools to help them detect change before it is on top of them. Because they live in a state of continuous change, they must also cultivate personal learning strategies that minimize the probability that their own skills will become automated (deeply rooted) unless those skills merit becoming so. These dynamic learners will be learning on the run and relying on Performance Support tools to assist them at every moment of learning, unlearning, and relearning. And when these dynamic learners see change coming at them, they will know how to assess their current readiness to perform and identify what skills and knowledge they need to cast aside. They will then determine how to take advantage of performer support systems to assertively adapt to the conditions around them.

IT'S BEST TO SOLVE WITH SELF-SUPPORT
AND COLLABORATION

One of the realities of life is that things don't always work the way they're supposed to work; life doesn't always happen according to a script. And sometimes, in our rapid pursuit of doing what we need to do, we make the wrong turn and experience those learning moments called *road blocks* or even failure. In the New Normal, it isn't enough to know how to do something correctly. It is also vital to be able to diagnose and solve problems that happen along the way. The situations we call "problems" can be caused by unforeseen circumstances, other people, and ourselves. Regardless of the source, these moments of Solve require diagnostic skills coupled with Performance Support.

The traditional organizational bandage for solving problems that arise in the workflow are "help desks" and sometimes intentionally created support networks—both backed by capable troubleshooters. When life was copasetic with only a few twists or turns along the way, this was a sufficient solution. But today, this model by itself won't solve the "solving" challenge. The New Normal has shifted the definition of competence from simply applying knowledge and skills to continually acquiring and adapting knowledge and skills. Competence is now a matter of individual learning agility, and the moments of Solve are prime contributors to the agility challenge.

Learners today must be comfortable in their ability to Solve unanticipated challenges. They must have confidence in the very act of not knowing. They must be disposed to face challenges beyond their current knowledge and skills. This confidence at these critical moments will come from the following:

- A Performance Support infrastructure that has anticipated their needs at the moment of Solve
- The training they have received to engage those tools in solving problems
- The on-the-job successes they have had along the way
- Organizational acceptance of failed attempts that may happen in the process

In addition, social media technologies provide remarkable opportunity for instantaneous access to the collective wisdom within and beyond the organizations we serve. Immediate collaboration at the moment of Solve and the capacity of individuals to resolve the core challenges that come their way combine to become the scalable resources that help desks need to meet the demands of the New Normal—a work environment in the state of constant flux.

HOW YOU CAN APPLY THIS:
CONDUCTING RAPID TASK ANALYSIS

Fundamental to any Performance Support strategy is the identification of the performance tasks the strategy needs to support. In addition, since tasks don't stand alone but actually orchestrate into higher workflow processes, a solid strategy also requires the determination of those processes. *Rapid task analysis* (RTA) is an approach for accomplishing this.

Rapid task analysis has three functional objectives:

1. Identify the job-specific tasks.
2. Identify related concepts.
3. Organize the tasks and concepts into meaningful business processes.

Functional Objective 1. Identify the Job-Specific Tasks

A *task* is a discrete set of steps that together achieve a specific outcome. For example, the following set of steps makes up the task of "Entering a phone number in your cell phone for quick dialing":

Step 1. Press the End button to clear all options.
Step 2. Press the right button under the menu option Names.
Step 3. Press the down arrow one time to highlight the menu option Add New.
Step 4. Press the left button under the menu option Select.

Step 5. Use the keypad to enter the name of the person whose number you will be adding.

Step 6. Press the left button under the menu option OK.

Step 7. Use the keypad to enter the phone number.

Step 8. Press the left button under the menu option OK.

During a rapid task analysis, you focus your efforts on identifying these tasks, not the steps. The steps are shown here to illustrate what a task is. Tasks have a discrete set of steps that accomplish a specific outcome.

Functional Objective 2. Identify Related Concepts

Where tasks describe how to do something, concepts provide the understanding behind those tasks. A *concept* is information that describes, at a minimum, what something is (and sometimes what it isn't) and why it is important. In addition, a concept may address who is influenced by it, when it may do that influencing, where the influencing takes place, and how often or how much. The only thing a concept doesn't address is how to do something.

For example, associated with the cell phone tasks of "Entering a phone number for quick dialing," "Quick dialing a call," and "Automatically entering the phone number of the person who just called you" is the concept of "quick dial options." This concept would include the following:

- Describe what "quick dial" is and the various quick dial options available. It could include an example in the form of an analogy or a scenario.
- Explain the benefits of these options.
- Describe situations in which these options are helpful.
- Provide related information such as the number of phone numbers that can be stored for quick dial.

All of these together would comprise the concept of "quick dial options."

Functional Objective 3. Organize the Tasks and Concepts into Meaningful Business Processes

Once you have identified all the tasks, you organize them into logical groupings called *processes*.

For example, in addition to "Entering a phone number for quick dialing," there is the related task of "Quick dialing a call." This task would automatically dial one of the numbers entered for quick dialing. Another task would be "Automatically entering the phone number of the person who just called you." These and other similar tasks would be considered a process.

RTA is rapid because it involves subject-matter experts who understand the work environment as well as the tools (such as software applications) that need to be used to complete specific job tasks. Using senior management executives (SMEs) eliminates the time-intensive requirement of the developer's becoming an SME. It is rapid also because it is a relatively simple, straightforward process that SMEs readily understand, and as a result they become more efficient over time in providing the information needed.

Rapid task analysis is not only helpful in developing your Performance Support strategy, it also provides you the scope and sequence for formal learning events. This outline can guide you throughout the development of all formal and informal learning solutions. Each process grouping (like the example above) contains a listing of concepts and tasks that should comprise a learning module. The RTA outline can also be used to guide your overall project planning and management. It can help SMEs provide focused assistance and content development. All in all, it is a fundamental practice that can bring continuity to all we do to support performers in all five of their moments of need.

For detailed instructions in conducting a rapid task analysis, see www.mhprofessional.com/InnovativePerformanceSuppport.

Analyzing Audiences

The results of your rapid task analysis set the stage for identifying all the audiences who will be performing each of the tasks and who must understand the requisite concepts. This doesn't take much time to do, but it must be done. What good is a listing of tasks and concepts if you don't map them to the performers you are charged to support? Table 2.2 gives a partial example of how the results of this analysis might look.

As you can see in Table 2.2, there are four job roles associated with the process "Sell and service the policy." Agents need to perform all eight tasks, but the district manager performs only four. And although the producers and licensed customer service representatives (CSRs) have the same tasks for this process, there are differences in other processes. If this weren't the case, these two audiences would merit being collapsed into a single audience. You want to map tasks and concepts only to the audiences that differ in their performance requirements. If, for example, there were no difference in task and concept requirements for producers and licensed CSRs, then they would comprise one audience rather than two.

Analyzing audiences doesn't take long to do, and it is most efficiently conducted as an activity at the completion of rapid task analysis.

Conducting Critical Skills Analysis

Skills vary in their importance and therefore merit different levels of attention across the five moments of need. For example, the task of "Setting up your e-mail contacts" is much less critical than "Securing your system against viruses." Obviously both skills merit attention, but the second task deserves greater investment in the grand scheme of things.

In order to establish an effective performer support strategy, you must know what the performances are that you need to support (identified via rapid task analysis), you must have those performances (tasks) mapped to audiences, and then you need to justify

Table 2.2. An Example of Mapping RTA Results to Performers

Tasks	Audience			
How to . . . Sell and Service the Policy	Agents	Producers	Licensed CSRs	District Manager
Help the customer choose an appropriate policy.	✓	✓	✓	✓
Create a quote.	✓	✓	✓	
Bind the policy (buy).	✓	✓	✓	
Edit the policy information.	✓	✓	✓	
Give instructions to the insured.	✓	✓	✓	✓
Cancel a policy.	✓	✓	✓	✓
Assist the customer with claims.	✓	✓	✓	✓
Get paid.	✓			✓

the allocation of learning and performer support resources for every audience for each task and associated concept. The approach for making this final assessment is called *critical skills analysis*.

Here's how you go about it:

Step 1. Establish a rating scale or set of scales that will help you assess the impact of failure if the task isn't completed successfully or the concept isn't understood. Table 2.3 gives an example of a rating scale for the question "How critical will the immediate impact of failure be to the organization?"

Table 2.3. An Example of a Rating Scale for Assessing the Impact of Failure

1	2	3	4	5	6	7
Not critical at all		Somewhat critical		Very critical		Absolutely critical

Step 2. Assign a failure impact rating for every task and concept for each audience. Table 2.4 gives an example.

Table 2.4. An Example of a Rating Scale Showing Impact Ratings

Critical Skills Impact Rating How to . . . Sell and Service the Policy	Audience			
	Agents	Producers	Licensed CSRs	District Manager
Help the customer choose an appropriate policy.	7	4	5	4
Create a quote.	7	4	5	
Bind the policy (buy).	7	7	7	
Edit the policy information.	5	3	6	
Give instructions to the insured.	5	4	4	5
Cancel a policy.	5	2	7	
Assist the customer with claims.	5	3	7	6
Get paid.	7			7

Step 3. Use these values to set your performer support strategy. In the example in Table 2.4, the task "Bind the policy (buy)" most likely merits a strong position in all five moments of need

whereas "Cancel a policy" for producers probably deserves treatment only by a job aid.

Obviously, common sense needs to always prevail, but a critical skills analysis combined with an RTA and audience analysis can provide you the information you need to invest your performer support efforts as wisely as possible.

INSIGHTS FROM A THOUGHT LEADER: Dr. Frank Nguyen

Dr. Frank Nguyen has managed the development and deployment of learning strategies and technologies for various Fortune 500 companies including American Express, Intel, and MicroAge. He was formerly an assistant professor in educational technology at San Diego State University, and he was voted the most influential faculty member in 2009. Dr. Nguyen has written various articles, books, and chapters on e-learning, instructional design, and Performance Support. His published work on Performance Support was recognized by the International Society for Performance Improvement (ISPI) with the 2008 Distinguished Dissertation Award. Dr. Nguyen has served on a variety of learning industry committees for Adobe, Brandon Hall, the American Society for Training and Development (ASTD), BJET, the eLearning Guild, and the ISPI.

Is Instructional Design Dead?

I have to confess. I have a warm soft spot in my heart for instructional design.

When I went back to graduate school many years ago, the first class I signed up for was called EDT 502: Introduction to Instructional Systems Design. Over the course of that semester, I learned the super secret language of instructional design (ID) like instructional objectives, assessments, alignment, and formative and summative evaluation. I was sold hook, line, and sinker.

My first years in the industry were spent as an instructional designer trying to make sense of a new (at least at the time) paradigm shift called "eLearning." Some years later, the first courses that I taught as a university professor were introductory and advanced instructional design courses. I have had the privilege of nurturing many instructional design professionals in both academic and industry settings.

Because of my ID roots, it pains me to admit that instructional design frankly isn't enough.

Gordon and Zemke (2000) published a *Training* magazine article a decade ago where they posed the provocative question, "Is instructional design dead?" They argued that instructional design was no longer relevant or effective. This sparked a debate that raged for a number of years, and the thread was recently revived in the blogosphere with ID supporters and skeptics lined up at opposite ends of the spectrum.

As with all things, the truth lies somewhere in the middle. For what it's worth, I don't think instructional design is dead. It's just no longer sufficient. The difference is subtle but important.

Looking at the Big Picture

Consider for a moment the field of astronomy. When most of us think of astronomy, we probably conjure up images of a lonely, solitary scientist toiling away late into the night (or early into the morning, depending in how you want to look at it). Astronomers are responsible for bringing us amazing images of galaxies that are said to be speeding away from us at speeds unimaginable. They tell us that the universe started in a single "big bang" that has since run amuck creating planets, stars, galaxies, and other objects floating around in space.

The funny thing is: you'd technically be wrong.

Strictly speaking, the literal translation of *astronomy* from its Greek roots is "law of the stars." At its inception, astronomy was limited to the study of what was then the known universe: the sun, other stars, planets, and the moon. It has since expanded to include comets, nebulae, clusters, and galaxies. In other words, astronomy is concerned with the design of any celestial object in the universe.

Big bang theory, the relationship between celestial objects, and the origin of the universe itself belongs to the relatively unknown field of cosmology. No, I'm not talking about doing a manicure or styling your hair (that's cosmetology, thank you very much). The literal translation of *cosmology* is "study of the universe." In other words, while an astronomer could tell you how a planetary system formed around a particular star, a cosmologist could tell you how its parent galaxy or even structure of the universe itself affected the formation of that particular planetary system. In short, astronomy is still a powerful and relevant science, but it is focused myopically on individual systems. Cosmology, on the other hand, looks at the big picture. It looks at the design of how those individual pieces interact together.

In many ways, instructional design is like astronomy. Despite the controversies and diverging opinions, it has proven itself over the past 50 years as a powerful and reliable methodology to create effective, repeatable learning events.

Designing Learning Experiences, Not Just Events

Instructor-led training (be it in a brick-and-mortar classroom or online) and Web-based training events will continue to be a staple in our diet, but we now have many other ingredients available to help us solve problems. But we have progressed beyond learning events.

For example, we can address communication issues through blogs, podcasts, e-mails, or even simple newsletters. We can capture the knowledge of experts or average employees using wikis. We can intelligently provide information to users through Performance Support embedded directly into the software tools they use on a daily basis. We can even provide real-time assistance to employees who may not be in a traditional office setting—such as equipment technicians, warehouse operators, or field sales representatives—through Performance Support integrated into mobile devices and smart phones.

The design of learning is no longer like astronomy. It should no longer be confined to myopic learning events that take place between the four walls of the classroom or virtually within the office cube. Learning is bigger than that. It can take place any time, anywhere, and we must design with that big picture in mind. The five moments of need provide us an excellent framework to comprehend this paradigm shift. While instructional design and learning events are squarely focused on the first two moments of need (learning for the first time and wanting to learn more), we need to be more mindful and deliberate with the other three moments of need.

Figure 2.2 illustrates one way to approach learning experience design. A learning experience can be split into three distinct phases: interventions that are delivered to an employee before a learning event, planned instruction and activities that occur during a learning event, and those that may occur sometime after the employee has returned to the workplace.

Instructional design teaches us to identify instructional objectives and then create instruction and practice to support those objectives. As shown in Figure 2.3, learning experience design starts at the end. We still need to determine the competencies and objectives that employees require to perform their job, but rather than starting off with training, we should seek to provide as much support as close to the work as possible. Our purpose as learning experience designers then is twofold: (1) to provide any information that the employee might require to perform the job on the job, and (2) to reinforce any learning that may occur within the Before or During phase of the learning experience. In this light, Performance Support plays a central role in this approach. The After phase may also include other interventions like coaching, mentoring, peer learning, or team activities to reinforce learning.

Once we've embedded as much learning in or near the work as possible, we can then focus on what interventions can be provided to employees before a learning event (see Figure 2.4).

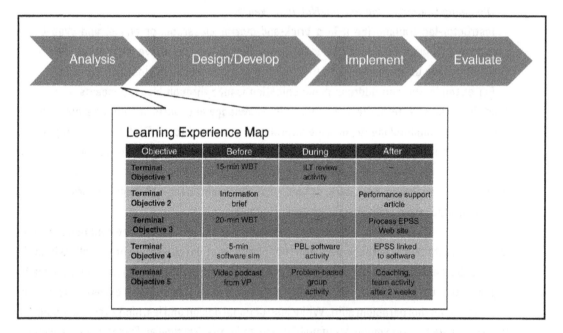

Figure 2.2. Using a Map to Design a Learning Experience before, during, and after a Training Event
Source: Dr. Frank Nguyen

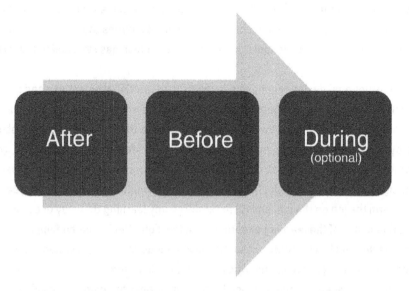

Figure 2.3. Learning Experience Design Starts with the End in Mind
Source: Dr. Frank Nguyen

Our purpose as designers in this phase is to provide information for instructional objectives that are foundational, may be used frequently by the employee, or that are critical to the employee, company, or customer. Interventions in the Before phase may include communications such as an e-mail from an executive or podcast from a subject-matter expert. In certain situations, the Before phase of a learning experience can be used to prepare employees in advance of a learning event. In ideal cases, a learning event may not even be necessary.

In the event that instructor-led training is still necessary, focusing on support after training and interventions beforehand allows an instructor and instructional designer to be more strategic. Rather than spending hours or days lecturing, classroom time can be spent instead on immersing learners in authentic problems. They can work individually or with their peers to

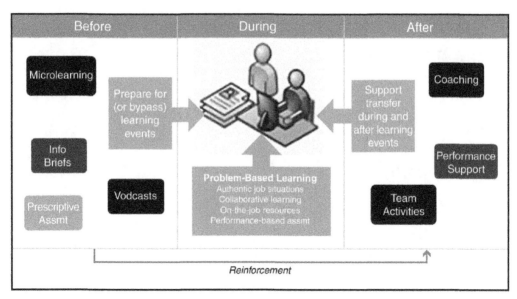

Figure 2.4. Learning Experience Example
Source: Dr. Frank Nguyen

solve issues they will likely face on the job. They can apply what they learned before the class in Web-based training or communications. They can also solve in-class problems using tools that will be available to them afterward such as Performance Support. Rather than designing inefficient learning events, we can maximize the investment in time between instructors and learners.

The Universe Is a Big Place

Cosmologists estimate that there are $9 \times 1{,}021$ (9 billion trillion) stars in the universe. It's hard to believe that up until a decade ago, our Sun was the only star with a known planetary system. In 1995, astronomers discovered the first planet outside of our solar system, also known as an *exoplanet*. As of June 2010, astronomers confirmed the existence of 461 exoplanets, and they have identified 706 other stars where exoplanets may exist. That still leaves roughly another 9 billion trillion stars to go (rounding up).

Like astronomers, we can no longer limit learning to small, myopic learning events. As such, we can no longer rely exclusively on instructional design. The universe is a big place, and planets can exist any time, anywhere. Learning is no different.

3

ESTABLISHING PROCESS AS YOUR LEARNING AND SUPPORT BACKBONE

If you can't describe what you are doing as a process, you don't know what you're doing.

—*W. Edwards Deming*

A STORY TO GET STARTED: WORKING SMART, FROM CON

I remember, as a ninth grader, sitting on the bench during the first basketball game of the season. At one point, Coach Fullmer sent me in to play. I had predetermined that when I got on the ball floor, I would work harder than anyone else. And I did just that. I ran hard chasing the ball wherever it was. Understandably, I didn't remain on the ball floor very long. I was quickly pulled back to the bench. I said to my coach, after sitting down, "Why did you pull me out? I was working harder than everyone else out there." Coach Fullmer's response was, "You were, but you weren't working very smart."

Today, more than ever before, organizations can't afford to waste effort. Process is what performers do independently and in concert with others in conducting the ongoing work of the organization. It requires a forward-moving integration of skills. A fundamental challenge of training is that it is altogether possible for performers to "master" all the tasks and concepts taught in a course and still emerge from the experience unable to integrate those independently mastered skills into their day-to-day workflow. The real world of work requires integration. Performance Support can and should be the primary means for ensuring this happens. But with this said, the journey of integrating skills into the workflow process begins during formal learning. This chapter addresses how you can and should establish process as your learning backbone so that everyone "works very smart" today and even smarter tomorrow. That's continuous performance improvement.

WHAT YOU NEED TO KNOW

When you add Performance Support to the mix, the pursuit of skill mastery changes. There are levels of mastery with Performance Support. Mastery obviously includes complete internalization of an independent skill. With this highest level of mastery a performer has the ability to complete a task automatically. This capacity is securely encoded into long-term memory and can be executed without conscience thought—it just happens when it needs to happen. On the other end of the mastery spectrum is the ability to efficiently complete a task using a job aid without any direct training on a specific skill. The successful use of the job aid is made possible by a generalizable understanding of how to use it.

Competency Achieved through Skill Integration
(Mastery versus Competency)

Competency embraces mastery at all its levels. But competence is only fully achieved when performers have integrated what they have mastered into actionable skill sets within the context of their personal workflow. This generally requires integration with other existing skill sets within the performer and also with other people via collaboration.

These integrated skill sets must be internalized at the appropriate level so they can be successfully executed as needed with a justifiable amount of effort. What is more, competency always carries with it sufficient conceptual understanding to facilitate proper judgment and the capacity to adapt, on the fly, to the unique challenges that occur in the workflow.

Here's an example:

There are six tasks and associated concepts taught in a course. If the performer masters these tasks independently, she has mastery but little competence. If she learns in the class how to integrate all six tasks into a workflow process, then competence begins to take root in the form of a *skill set*. This skill set expands competency as it is integrated with other skill sets initially learned in other classes and honed by real-world experience. Organizational competency happens as people begin working together by blending their skill sets together in collaborative work. (See Figure 3.1.)

Here's another example to illustrate further:

Suppose you completed a course titled "Mastering Spreadsheets." The course was facilitated by a remarkable instructor who taught

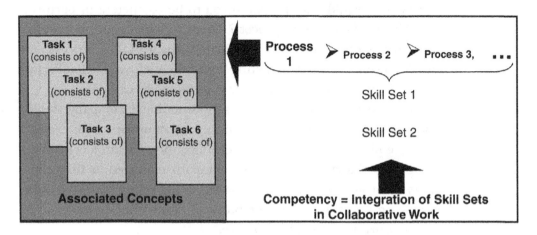

Figure 3.1. Competency Achieved through Skill-Set Integration

you all the details for using your organization's spreadsheet software. During the class, you practiced and mastered 10 fundamental skills associated with that software. Suppose also that your day-to-day work doesn't require you to use that software but you do need to use it as part of periodic ongoing project work with others in your organization. In this work, you receive digital spreadsheets from three other work groups, and you do the following:

1. Consolidate those spreadsheets.
2. Add specific data, gathered from several other applications to the now-combined set of spreadsheets.
3. Perform a number of calculations.
4. Make judgments based on those calculations.
5. Enter those judgments into another application along with specific data points.
6. Forward the revised spreadsheets to other members of your work team.
7. Monitor the completion of your team members' calculations.
8. Reconcile any discrepancies in their conclusions via a virtual meeting.

Question: To what degree do you think the Mastering Spreadsheets class would have prepared you to be competent in performing this specific workflow process? There's a high chance it wouldn't have unless the course had anticipated this workflow process and provided you practice completing it and then left you with a Performance Support tool to help you at your moments of Apply.

We once were asked to help a multinational company design and implement an enterprise training solution for an enterprise-resource-planning (ERP) reengineering effort. The project involved completely changing the way the company managed its financials. Every associated workflow process was being redesigned to involve people on the front line of the business who had never engaged in the organization's financials before.

We opted to train on business processes. We linked business and nonbusiness tasks with workflows and job roles. We developed a Web-based Performance Support system that provided access to specific task instructions via role-based online workflow diagrams. We used the online system as the primary training resource in every class. Our objective was to train all of the participants to use the online Performance Support system to help them do their job.

The result? The go-live day was a nonevent. We had put extra support personnel at the help desk, but by the third day we sent the extra help back to their work areas because they weren't needed. The company had completely changed how several thousand people performed their jobs without a hiccup. Why? Because workflow process was the backbone of the training effort coupled with a Web-based *Performance Support broker* that supported those processes.

Workflow process is the primary means for ensuring that performance is purposefully and effectively directed. It should be the backbone of all training and Performance Support efforts.

Research-Proven Principles That Support Using Process in Performance Support

The following four principles support the use of process as the backbone of your training and Performance Support efforts.

Principle 1. Encode with Process to Facilitate More Efficient Retrieval

Here's a test. From memory do the following as fast as you can:

1. Recite every third month in the year followed by every second month in a year.
2. Recite the letters of the alphabet backward by every other letter.

Now do the following:

1. Recite the months of the year in sequential order.
2. Recite the letters of the alphabet in sequential order.

If you're normal, assignments 1 and 2 were much more challenging than assignments 3 and 4. This is because of how you encoded the months of the year and the letters of the alphabet into your long-term memory. *Encoding* is the process by which knowledge and skills are transferred from short-term memory to long-term memory. The point of this activity is to demonstrate that the way performers encode knowledge and skills influences the way they are best able to retrieve the same knowledge and skills. Since you most likely encoded the months of the year and the letters of the alphabet sequentially, your ability to retrieve that information is most efficiently accomplished by retrieving it sequentially.

Now, with the above exercise in mind, consider how skills for the workplace should be best encoded. Clearly it should be done according to how performers most likely would retrieve those skills. And when it comes to the workplace, people are applying what they have learned during the flow of their work. Workflow process, then, is the best way to encode skills. There are other options for encoding a set of tasks. A different option would be to train according to the menu structure of a software package. This most likely would differ from the workflow. This wouldn't be as effective in terms of retrieval. Doing this would present a challenge similar to the first two memory retrieval challenges you faced at the beginning of this section (for example, "Recite the letters of the alphabet backward by every other letter").

Principle 2. Provide Meaningful Context

In December 2009, a team of researchers from the University of Toronto and the Krembil Neuroscience Centre at the University Health Network reported in the *Proceedings of the National Academy of Sciences* (at www.pnas.org) that the hippocampus, a brain region in the temporal lobe, employs context cues to initiate recall from long-term memory. This study is significant because it established that it is not only the strength of memory that facilitates retrieval but context as well.

Research on the role of context in learning reinforces the previous principle. In the world of work, context is defined by the flow of work. When workflow process is the backbone during the encoding (learning) stage, then what is learned can be retrieved readily as performers engage in their workflow—especially when there is Performance Support tightly aligned with the same workflow.

Principle 3. Associate with Existing Skill Sets

Skills and knowledge tend to make the journey into long-term memory more readily when they are associated with related skills and information already there. And although we can't be sure if anything is ever really lost from long-term memory, all of us have experienced a *memory blank*. This is where we know we know something (like someone's name) but we can't seem to remember it.

When new learning is tightly (logically) linked to old learning, these linkages can ensure its retrieval more quickly. If you want rapid learning and quick recall, then make sure you establish logical linkage with knowledge and skills previously learned, and reinforce that linkage in how you organize your Performance Support solutions.

Principle 4. Use Workflow Visuals to Help Performers Build Mental Models

Mental models are *memory structures* that facilitate thinking and help manage the integration of new learning with prior learning. These structures are stored in long-term memory and facilitate more efficient retrieval of information from long-term memory into working memory where they can assist thinking and help solve problems. These memory structures then provide the framework for encoding new understanding back into long-term memory.

Visual depictions of workflows, when designed and implemented properly, can help performers establish effective mental models. As you read through the rest of this chapter, you will learn how to do this.

What a Process Backbone Looks Like

Figure 3.2 shows the home screen for a digital Performance Support tool that has organized its support content according to a workflow process. This first screen shows the overarching business process that engages four different job roles.

The Process tab in the top left of the menu ribbon provides performers the option to access specific Performance Support content for each of the tasks shown in this job requisition process.

The menu ribbon also provides access to role-specific tasks (for example, hiring manager, recruiter, senior management, and human resources).

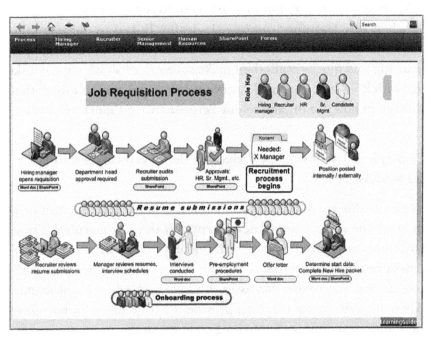

Figure 3.2. A Digital Performance Support Tool: The Overarching Business Process That Engages Four Job Roles

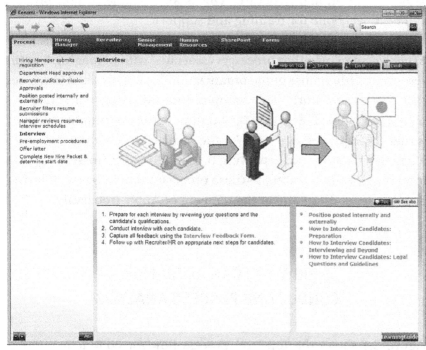

Figure 3.3. A Digital Performance Support Tool: The Role-Specific Tasks

When the performer clicks on the left Process tab, a screen appears, like the one in Figure 3.3. Directly under the Process tab is a listing of each of the process tasks (shown graphically in the previous screen). In this example the "Interview" task is selected. To the right of the listing of tasks is a graphic showing where the interview fits in the workflow along with the specific steps for interviewing listed just below the graphic. This screen also contains links to specific resources the hiring manager needs to successfully complete these steps.

In this example, all of the content is organized, primarily, according to how hiring managers, recruiters, senior management, and the human resources people work together to recruit employees. Best practice would use this process as the organizational structure for training people with these job roles. During the training, they would be trained to use this Performance Support tool as they move through the workflow process. The training flow would follow this same organizational structure. This is an example of how process can be a backbone for training and support.

The job requisition process shown in Figures 3.2 and 3.3 is most likely one of many other processes associated with managing human resources. Other parts of the organization have their set of processes that drive their work (for example, finance, sales, marketing, or manufacturing). The key understanding to derive from this chapter is that these processes should be the means for encoding skills into long-term memory and retrieving those skills. Performance Support tools organized according to those processes should be used during training (encoding) and at the moment of Apply (retrieval.)

HOW YOU CAN APPLY THIS:
CONDUCTING PROCESS ANALYSIS

Figure 3.4 shows the top-level process flow for conducting *process analysis*. Behind each of the darkest process boxes are second-level process flows. The lightest boxes represent tasks. Each of these three primary process paths are described below.

Process Path 1. Complete Rapid Task Analysis

This first process is iterative since it is possible that a process analysis may involve the results of multiple RTAs. Process often addresses a broader view than what is covered by a single RTA session. The decision point following this first process provides this expansion option.

As you can see in Figure 3.5, the RTA process has three subprocesses. The RTA checklist (found online at www.mhprofessional .com/InnovativePerformanceSuppport) lists the tasks for each of these processes. Chapter 2 also provides information regarding how to conduct an RTA. Figure 3.6 shows the tasks for each of these processes.

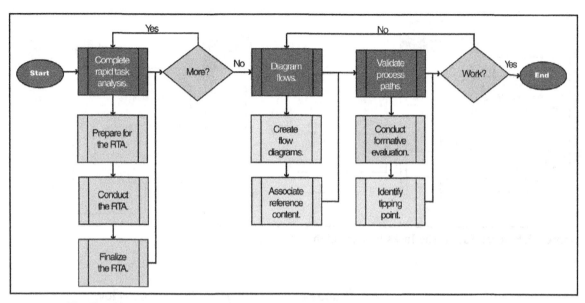

Figure 3.4. The Top-Level Process Flow for Conducting Process Analysis

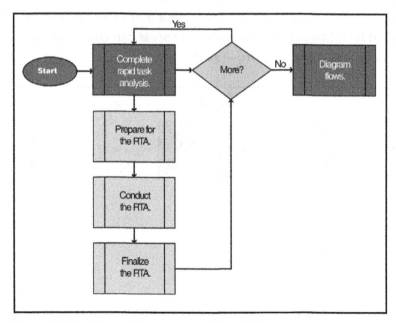

Figure 3.5. The Three Subprocesses of the RTA

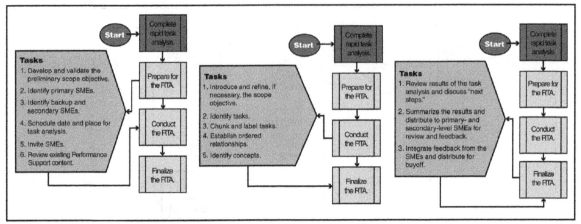

Figure 3.6. Process Path 1. The Tasks for Each of the RTA Subprocesses

Process Path 2. Diagram the Process Flows

As shown in Figure 3.7, this second process has two tasks (unlike the first, which had three subprocesses). Each of these tasks can be completed by following a set of steps. A process can consist of other processes or tasks, or a mixture of both.

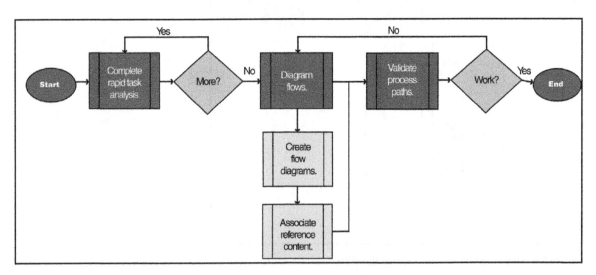

Figure 3.7. Process Path 2. The Two Tasks for Diagraming Process Flows

Task 1. Create Flow Diagrams

The steps for creating your workflow diagrams are given in Table 3.1.

Table 3.1. Steps for Creating Workflow Diagrams

	Step		Comments
1	Diagram the process level closest to the tasks identified during RTA.		• At the completion of an RTA, you have a set of processes composed of tasks (called *edge processes*). In this step you create a diagram showing how each of these edge processes fit together in an overarching workflow. • Depending on the number of edge processes and the nature of the work, there may be more than one process flow.
2	IF	the edge processes merit diagramming, do so.	• Generally the edge processes merit diagramming. • If there are only a few tasks in each of the edge processes and if they lack decision points, branching, or a workflow logic, then the edge processes may not merit diagramming.
3	IF	there is more than one process flow developed in step 1, diagram the next process level.	• If, when you complete this step, there is more than one process flow at this level, then create a process flow for the next. • The key here is to keep rolling up processes until you have a single process flow at the top of the process hierarchy.

Task 2. Associate Reference Content

Reference content includes information regarding audiences or roles, related concepts, and support tools. The steps for completing this task are given in Table 3.2.

Table 3.2. Steps for Associating Reference Content

	Step	Comments
1	Associate audiences with the process flows.	• See the section on conducting audience analysis in Chapter 2. • If needed, distinguish those with primary from those with secondary responsibility.
2	Associate concepts at the appropriate levels of the process flows.	• The concepts were identified during the RTA. Here you map those concepts at the most relevant points of the workflow diagrams. • A concept can map to multiple points at multiple levels.
3	Associate support tools and reference content at the relevant points at each process flow level.	• These tools may include forms, job aids, checklists, and so on. • Reference content could be in the form of video, documents, or other media.

Process Path 3. Validate the Process Paths

Figure 3.8 shows the flow for this process. Further below is a description of two potential tasks you can complete (via traditional formative evaluation practices) to validate your process paths. Below that is a singular task that is more readily completed during this validation process.

Process: Conduct Formative Evaluation

Formative evaluation is a fundamental instructional development practice. It is a process because there are a number of tasks associated with it. Table 3.3 briefly describes two tasks that are relevant for validating process paths.

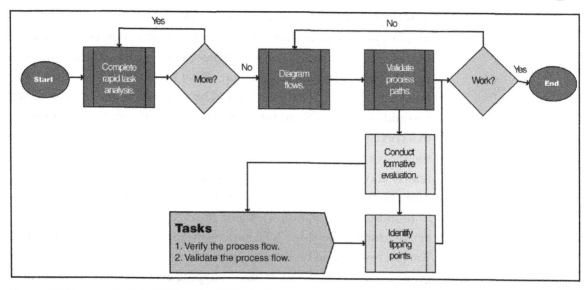

Figure 3.8. Process Path 3. Validate the Process Paths

Table 3.3. Two Tasks That Are Completed During Formative Evaluation

	Task	Comments
1	Verify the process flows.	• Distribute the process flows to the appropriate SMEs to verify its completeness and accuracy.
2	Validate the process flows.	• The previous task can help provide a beginning validation, but verifying that the process flows are accurate doesn't necessarily mean that they are helpful.
		• This step determines that they have been designed in such a way that they actually help people as they learn and during their work.
		• This step is best accomplished by having actual performers move through the processes in their places of work.

Task: Identify Tipping Points

Often, in processes there are key *tipping points* (that is, transition points) at which it becomes costly if not impossible to undo what has been done. For example, we often host our clients at the Sundance

Resort in Utah. The team members generally stay at a cabin there, and we spend several days working on strategic issues. During at least one of the breakfasts, we cook whole-wheat waffles. During the process of cooking those waffles, whole-wheat kernels are ground into fine flour. The grinding into flour would be a tipping point—at that point it would be impossible to return the flour into the state it was in prior to its being ground. Later in the recipe, egg whites are separated from the yolks and whipped. Ingredients are mixed together and then ultimately cooked in a waffle iron. Then, of course, they're eaten. In the case of waffles, every event can be classified as a tipping point.

In most typical workflows, there aren't many tipping points. For example, during the three RTA processes, there isn't one tipping point. You can reverse and revise at any point. However, when you update your general ledger, there is most likely a tipping point or two in the journey.

These tipping points merit identification and special treatment in training and in Performance Support. This is not a complex task. Table 3.4 gives the steps for addressing this unique challenge.

Designing Effective Process Flows

Here are five guiding principles to help you design effective process flows.

Table 3.4. Steps for Identifying Tipping Points

	Steps	Comments
1	Send a copy of the process flows to appropriate SMEs.	You can include this task when you distribute the process flows to SMEs in step 1 of process 3.
2	Explain to the SMEs what a tipping point is.	A *tipping point* is any step, task, or process within the process flows at which there is a transition that has high impact, where it is costly or difficult to undo what has been done.
3	Ask the SMEs to identify the tipping points in the process flows with a brief rationale.	The rationale should include why it is a tipping point, and it should state the consequences if that transition is made improperly.

Principle 1. For Collaborative Processes, Visually Depict Who Does What When

Figure 3.9 shows how this can be done by providing a *role key* and then visually showing at each point of the process who is involved. This example also uses graphics effectively to depict what people are doing at each point in the process.

Principle 2. When Possible, Provide Contextual Links to Resources at Relevant Points of the Flow

In Figure 3.9, there are seven buttons under specific points in the process flow. Clicking on the buttons provides access to resources that support that specific process point.

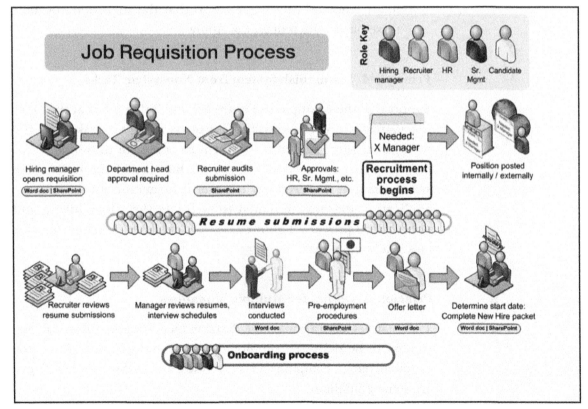

Figure 3.9. An Effective Depiction of Who Does What When

Principle 3. Provide Enough Text to Ensure Clarity

Again, in Figure 3.9 the descriptions are, for the most part, intuitive. Here are a few guidelines:

- Make sure the process label conveys that someone is "doing" something. For example "Hiring manager opens requisition" or "HR, senior management, and others give approvals" rather than "Approvals: HR, senior management, and others."
- Be consistent with your label style. Table 3.5 shows how the labels in Figure 3.9 could be made more consistent.
- Number your process points. Numbering helps performers know how big the process is. It also helps with encoding if there is a hierarchical sequence that must be followed. For example, if step 2 needs to be completed prior to step 3, the numbering helps "encode" that sequence so that the steps don't become mixed-up at the moment of Apply.

Principle 4. Distinguish System from Nonsystem Tasks

Suppose in the example in Figure 3.9 and Table 3.5 that the "Hiring manager opens requisition" process had four tasks that the hiring manager needed to perform to complete it. Suppose further that three were nonsystem tasks but one of the tasks was a *system task* that required her to enter information into a software application that was designed to facilitate the entire hiring and onboarding process. The process flow needs to indicate that this task is a "system task."

Principle 5. Design for Multiple Modalities

The realities of training and Performance Support often call for content to be delivered simultaneously in multiple modalities (for example, paper, computer screens, slides, and mobile devices). Here are some guidelines:

Table 3.5. How to Make Labels More Consistent

	Current Label	Better Label	Comments
1	None	The Requisitioning Jobs process begins.	There are two processes shown here. This label provides consistency with the second "macro" process label below.
2	Hiring manager opens requisition.	None	This is the standard style for other labels to match (role + verb + object). The role is listed up front because the only distinguishing element for the role icons is their color and not all people will see the colors to make the distinctions. If this weren't a collaborative process with multiple roles, then the format would be verb + object (for example, giving approval).
3	Department head approval required.	Department head gives approval.	This better label conveys what needs to happen for the process to continue.
4	Recruiter audits submission.	None	
5	Approvals: HR, senior management, and others.	HR, senior management, and others give approvals.	
6	Recruitment process begins.	The Recruiting New Employees process begins.	This is the starting label for a new "macro" process.
7	Position posted internally and externally.	Recruiter and hiring manager post position (internally and externally).	Consistency is more important than brevity.
8	Résumé submissions.	Candidates submit résumés.	The original label is a common practice, but such labels fail to explicitly convey "doing."

Note: For practice, review the remaining six processes, and determine how they could be brought to greater consistency.

- **Design to minimize multidirectional scrolling.** The direction of a flow can become a problem if performers are required to follow the flow by scrolling beyond the screen in two directions in order to comprehend the flow (for example, scrolling left to right and scrolling top to bottom). Although the example in Figure 3.10 has a top-level process flow running left to right and a subprocess flow running top to bottom, there isn't a need to scroll in both directions. The limited amount of text in the boxes and the limited number of boxes in each of the five paths dropping down from the top process allow the performer to see it all and only scroll left to right. As long as this holds true across all the modalities where the process flows will be deployed, then you are following this guideline.

- **For complex flows with three or more levels, consider providing context maps to keep performers from getting lost.** Figure 3.11 shows the third-level process flow. Context is maintained by keeping the top-level flow and dropping out the second-level

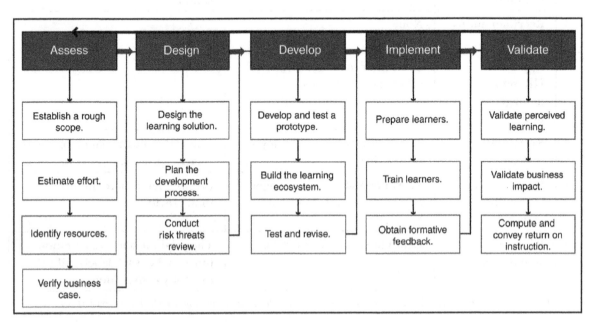

Figure 3.10. A Design That Minimizes Multidirectional Scrolling

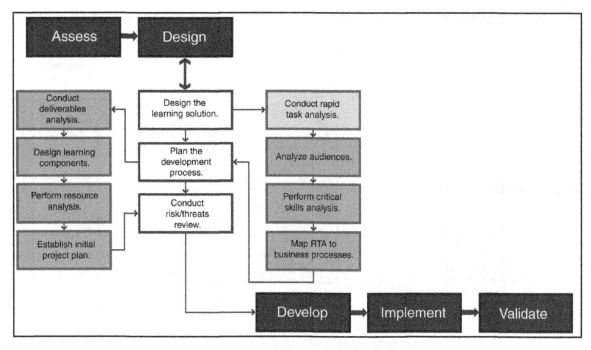

Figure 3.11. The Third-Level Process Flow

flows except the flow that leads to the third-level processes. With the exception of rapid task analysis, all other boxes left and right are tasks. The RTA has three subprocesses, each leading to a set of tasks. Figure 3.12 shows how a context map might look for the three processes associated with the RTA.

At the beginning of this chapter, we said that competence is fully achieved only when performers have integrated what they have mastered into actionable skill sets. This generally requires integration with other existing skill sets within the performer and also with other people via collaboration.

How you visually depict the workflows that describe the processes you are supporting will help or hinder this integration.

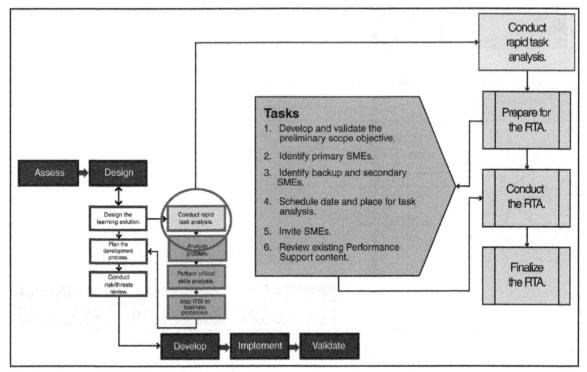

Figure 3.12. A Context Map for Three Processes Associated with the RTA

INSIGHTS FROM A THOUGHT LEADER: Dr. Ruth Clark

Dr. Ruth Clark is the principal and president of CLARK Training & Consulting. A recognized specialist in instructional design and technical training, Dr. Clark holds a doctorate in educational psychology and instructional technology from the University of Southern California. Prior to founding CLARK Training & Consulting, Dr. Clark served as training manager for Southern California Edison. She is a past president of the International Society for Performance Improvement (ISPI). Ruth is the author of six books on evidence-based learning including her recent book Evidence-based Training Methods *and the bestseller* e-Learning and the Science of Instruction *with Dr. Richard Mayer.*

Dr. Clark is the 2006 recipient of the Thomas F. Gilbert Distinguished Professional Achievement Award from ISPI, and she was a Training Legend Speaker at the 2007

American Society for Training and Development (ASTD) International Conference and Expo (ICE) event. For over 20 years, Ruth has worked as an independent consultant offering workshops, keynotes, and consulting on design and development of workforce learning environments for classroom, asynchronous e-learning, and the virtual classroom.

Cognitive Learning Models

Source: Adapted from Ruth Clark's articles for this book.

Current theories of learning are based on the interaction among three memory systems and the processes that move information among them.

The Three Memory Systems

The three memory systems are the visual and auditory sensory memories, working or short-term memory, and long-term memory. First, data from the eyes and ears are temporarily stored in visual and auditory sensory memory, and then they move into working (short-term) memory. Working memory is a limited-capacity processor that includes separate storage for auditory and visual information. One landmark in the development of cognitive psychology was the classic paper by Miller, who referred to the capacity of working memory as "7 plus or minus 2."[1] Working memory, while limited in capacity, is the central processor for learning and thinking. For learning to occur, new sensory information from the visual and auditory systems must be integrated in working memory to form a coherent idea. Then these ideas must be rehearsed in working memory in a way that integrates new ideas into existing memories (called *schemas*) in long-term memory. The integration of new data into existing schemas is called *encoding*. Long-term memory has a large storage capacity. However, encoding into long-term memory is not sufficient. Because all processing takes place in working memory, the new knowledge and skills encoded into long-term memory must be retrieved into working memory when needed to perform a skill or task. This final stage is the cognitive basis for transfer of learning.

Cognitive Processes Involved in Learning: Overview

There are several critical processes that mediate the processes behind transformation of sensory data into retrievable knowledge in long-term memory. They include attention, rehearsal in working memory, retrieval from long-term memory, and metacognitive monitoring. Because working memory has a limited capacity and accepts data from the environment and from long-term memory, attention is the psychological mechanism used to narrow incoming information to accommodate limits of working memory. It is important that student attention be focused on elements in the environment that are relevant to learning and filter out irrelevant elements. Providing cueing devices, such as arrows or bolding of text in instructional materials, and providing instructional objectives are two instructional techniques that support attention.

New sensory data entering working memory from the visual and auditory sensory memories must be integrated, first, with each other to form coherent ideas and integrated, second, into existing schema in long-term memory. Instructional events that activate relevant prior knowledge in long-term memory and stimulate rehearsal in working memory support these integrations. When new knowledge and skills are needed later on the job, retrieval from long-term memory during learning into working memory is essential to the transfer of learning. Retrieval requires that cues the learner will encounter in the work environment be encoded in new schema at the time of learning. Therefore, a lesson that teaches how to take a blood-pressure measurement must use the blood-pressure equipment during learning so that the right cues are available later when the learner needs to take a blood-pressure reading on the job. Finally, metacognition serves as the operating mechanism for learning. Metacognitive skills are responsible for setting learning goals, determining learning strategies, monitoring progress, and making adjustments as needed. Learners with undeveloped metacognitive skills profit from high instructional structure and support in managing and monitoring their learning. For example, frequent skills tests to assess knowledge help these learners spot topics that require additional study.

Construction of Knowledge

Cognitive models of instruction view learning as a process that requires learners to actively construct new knowledge. The role of instruction is to provide an environment that helps the learner leverage the cognitive processes summarized earlier and minimize their disruption. Specifically, instruction should help the learner in these ways:

- Focus attention to elements of the environment relevant to learning
- Minimize cognitive load in order to use the limited resources of working memory most effectively
- Rehearse new information in working memory so that it is integrated into existing schemas in long-term memory

- Retrieve new knowledge when needed after the learning
- Manage and monitor the metacognitive learning processes

Managing Cognitive Load in Working Memory

After new data from the environment enter working memory, they must be processed. Specifically, auditory and visual data must be integrated into a coherent idea. And new ideas must be integrated with preexisting knowledge stored in long-term memory schemas. All of this processing activity requires capacity in working memory. Because working memory is a limited-capacity processor, instructional techniques that reduce cognitive load have been proven to improve learning effectiveness and efficiency. This is especially true of novice learners, who are most susceptible to cognitive overload.

Numerous load-management techniques have been reported in recent literature.[2] We describe several here, including the modality principle and the contiguity principle.

The Modality Principle

Mayer[3] and Clark and Mayer[4] derived a number of principles for the development of lesson materials based on controlled experiments that measured learning from the study of instructional materials (books or multimedia) teaching scientific processes. The *modality principle* asks the question, "Is learning better when instructional visuals are described with text or with audio narration?" A number of experiments in which multimedia lessons teaching scientific processes, such as how a bolt of lightening forms or how a brake works, used animation explained either by text or by the same words delivered in audio narration. The materials using audio to describe the words resulted in an 80 percent median gain in learning, for an effect size of 1.17. Mayer concluded that learning is deeper when the limited capacity of working memory is maximized by coordinated inputs into the visual and auditory subsystems rather than just into the visual subsystem, as is the case when text is used to describe visuals.[5]

The Contiguity Principle

When designing instruction materials or Web-based instruction in which bandwidth precludes the use of audio, graphics must be explained by text. In these situations, a number of researchers have shown that integrating the text into the graphic is better than separating the text. For example, in demonstrating a geometry problem solution in text, Sweller et al. found that an integrated version, in which the problem steps are placed into the geometry illustration, produced better learning than the same steps placed underneath the illustration.[6] Mayer found similar results with placement of text adjacent to or distant from illustrations in multimedia lessons.[7] From comparisons in five experiments, Mayer found a median gain in learning of 68 percent, with an effect size of 1.12 for lessons that integrated text into illustrations. Less mental effort is involved in the integration of pictures and text when they are placed physically close to each other on the page or screen. Mayer referred to this as the *contiguity principle of instruction.*

4

BEGINNING AT THE MOMENT OF APPLY AND DESIGNING FROM THERE

Many things difficult to design prove easy to perform.
—Samuel Johnson

A STORY TO GET STARTED:
BUILDING WITHOUT DESIGN, FROM CON

My father and I added a storage room onto the basement of our home at the request of my mother. We figured that we could do it even though we had never done anything like it before. In my home town of Circleville, there weren't any restrictions for projects like this. So we had Shirl Fox drop by with his backhoe and dig a hole next to the house where we thought the room ought to be. The Dalton Brothers brought a load of cement and dropped it in the bottom of the hole for a floor. We asked Johnson Ruby to stop by and show us how to lay the cinderblock (he instructed us right at the moment of Apply). The Dalton Brothers brought over another load of cement, and we capped the roof with it. I then knocked a hole through the wall in the basement for the door. Seemed pretty straightforward to us. We had no real training to do any of it, and we hadn't drawn up any plans beforehand. We just built it.

When we finally showed Mom the room, she pointed out a few flaws. First, the floor of the storage room was six inches lower than the rest of the basement (we hadn't planned that). The walls of the storage room were a bit off kilter, and there was groundwater seeping into the room from the drain we had put in. It took some time for us to get the room into a state in which Mom would store anything in it, and in reality it wasn't ever the storage room it needed to be.

Sadly, this is the way many organizations build their Performance Support solutions. They are generally created after the development of the training solution. Often, there isn't much, if any, upfront design; they're simply patterned after other Performance Support solutions. The result? Something that works like the room Dad and I built: It looks like a job aid, but it doesn't quite do all it could do if it had been designed properly.

WHAT YOU NEED TO KNOW

This chapter introduces design principles and a development strategy that will help you build effective Performance Support solutions.

Sidekicks, Planners, and Quick-Checks

Chapter 2 introduced the three time phases of Apply: the time before performance, the time during performance, and the time after performance ends.

The *time during performance* has been the primary focus of Performance Support for decades. Allison Rossett, in her book *Job Aids and Performance Support: Moving from Knowledge in the Classroom to Knowledge Everywhere,* has called the solutions we build to support performers during this moment of time "sidekicks." One example of a sidekick is an online help system that provides the steps to follow while completing a specific task. Another example might be a checklist to guide sales representatives while they are speaking with potential customers via the phone.

Rossett has also introduced another time phase of Apply: the need to plan prior to actually performing. She calls these kinds of performer support solutions "planners." In the real world, there are instances in which it would be inappropriate or even improbable to reference a PS solution during the actual moment of Apply.

For example, suppose you took a training course to help you develop the skills you need to respond to a disgruntled employee. Now, over a year later, you receive your first call from an employee who is upset with the company and considering legal action. Since taking the course, there has been new legislation regarding how organizations must respond to the issues raised by the employee. You have 30 minutes to prepare for the interview. What do you do?

This is when a "planner" would prove very helpful. It could provide you the option to review, at a high level, the principles introduced in the course with links to all legal guidelines including highlighting those that have changed since you took the course. This performer support planner might also provide you the option to dive deeper into any principle including viewing e-learning video bursts demonstrating each of the principles. There could also be a planning tool that helped create a tailored agenda to guide you and the employee through the meeting. All of this would support performance prior to your actually conducting the interview.

The third time phase of Apply is a critical area for any organization interested in continuous performance improvement. In this phase, following the actual act of Apply, performers conduct an assessment called a *quick-check*. Here the performer support strategy might include tools and processes to facilitate the assessment. For example, in the previous example, following the meeting with the disgruntled employee, you might move through a checklist to identify which principles you employed and others you might also have used. You might also summarize any lessons you learned and how you might improve your performance. This note would be available for you to review when you conducted your next interview with the same or another disgruntled employee. Quick-checks are the newest practice areas of performer support, and they merit full attention.

To help you design effective Performance Support solutions regardless of whether or not you are supporting performance before, during, or following the moment of Apply, determine which of the five moments of need merit support during each of the time phases. Performers may simply need help performing the task, remembering a concept, or accessing other information that will help them do what they need to do. But, as mentioned in Chapter 2, during the moment of Apply, performers may also need to learn something New, learn More about something, adapt to Change, or Solve a problem.

Table 4.1 provides an overview of questions to help you make this initial assessment. These questions will be addressed in greater detail in the chapter sections that follow.

Overarching Design Principles

An effective job aid requires more than the right content in the right form (for example, paper, mobile device, or Web page). A job aid is usable to the degree that it can be readily scanned, quickly read, and comprehended appropriately. If performers must labor to achieve this, many will opt to go elsewhere for their Performance Support. There is much you can do to help performers rapidly grasp what they need to obtain from a job aid. Typography and graphics can help performers achieve greater understanding in less time if used appropriately. The page layout or grid can affect usability for better or worse depending on the decisions you make.

Even if you write well, you should design the typography, graphics, and grid to enhance the usability of your job aids. If it all appears uninviting to your readers, they may never take time to use it. To make a job aid as usable as possible, you should take the following steps:

- Incorporate structured writing.
- Write simply.
- Use typography to enhance readability.
- Establish proper graphic conventions.

Table 4.1. An Overview of Some of the Questions to Answer in Designing Support Solutions

Moment of Need	Is There a Need for Support *before* Performance? (Planners)	Is There a Need for Support *during* Performance? (Sidekicks)	Is There a Need for Support *after* Performance? (Quick-Checks)
Apply	Do performers need help remembering specific tasks? Do performers need help remembering specific concepts? Is there information performers need to review? Would a planning tool be useful?	Do performers need help remembering and/or completing specific tasks (system, nonsystem, principle governed)? Are there tasks that independently merit real-time support? Do performers need access to information? Do performers need access to specific tools?	Is there justification for individual pursuit of ongoing performance improvement? Is there opportunity for peer evaluation? Is there a need to capture lessons learned? Is there capability to capture performance for a postevaluation?
Change	Has there been any change in performance requirements? Is there new or updated information?	Has there been any change in performance requirements? Is there new or updated information?	Should performers determine personal performance gaps?
Solve	Are there potential problems and/or challenges that require planning? Should lessons learned be available as planners?	Are there potential problems and/or challenges?	Is the determination of problem resolution counterintuitive? Is there ongoing value in capturing solutions with lessons learned?
Learn New	Will there be performers who haven't participated in formal training in this area?	Will there be performers who haven't participated in formal training in this area?	Are there learning outcomes that merit the investment in performance assessment?
Learn More	Do aspects of the performance requirements call for additional training?	Do aspects of the performance requirements call for additional training?	Are there learning outcomes that merit the investment in performance assessment?

Incorporate Structured Writing

How you structure information on a page or screen influences the ability of readers to access and process information. *Structured writing* is a method of organizing information to facilitate performers' searching for information, seeing the relationships of information, and then using it.

Titles, headers, and footers should provide critical reference points for performers, allowing rapid recognition of what the job aid is and how it interconnects with their broader world of performance—especially in the context of their workflow.

Margin space with callouts and headings can also facilitate timely information access. In addition, tables can allow the creation of consistent *content maps* where a type of information is consistently structured in tabular form. Once performers understand how the information is structured, they will be able to use the structure to more readily scan and then process the information once they find it.

Fundamental to structured writing is the identification of the different types of content and the establishment of a consistent grid for portraying that content. For example, as shown in Figure 4.1, you may choose to create a two-column grid for step-by-step instructions, a three-column table for a procedure overview, and a single-column grid with margin callouts (with headings, term definitions, and summaries) for text-intensive job aids. As long as you establish consistent grids for each type of content, performers will use the grids to access and process information efficiently.

To incorporate structured writing in your job aids, consider following these general guidelines:

- Keep headers and footers simple.
  - o Include page numbers, chapter numbers and titles, and when appropriate, section numbers and titles.
  - o Include information that will help performers search through the document, understand where they are in context of the entire document, and identify updated portions of the document.

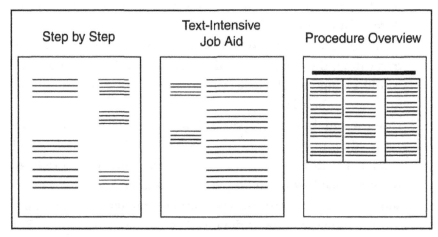

Figure 4.1. Possible Grids for Content Presentations

    o Place search information in the outer corners of the pages.
- Keep wide margins for headings, summaries, and definitions.
- Create a consistent typography and grid for each type of content and form.

Write Simply

Pascal, a French mathematician, once apologized for writing a lengthy letter by saying that he hadn't time to write a shorter one. Good writing is always simple. But the time constraints of developing Performance Support make it difficult. Here are three general guidelines, in the form of questions you can ask of your own writing:

1. Can I omit it and still communicate the idea? The first key to simple writing is removal. Don't get emotionally attached to the words you write. You may have worked hard to craft a set of words into an idea, but if the idea isn't a critical contributor, omit it.
2. Can I simplify and/or standardize words or phrases? Although you may not be able to omit a word, it often merits simplification or standardization. Although little needs to be said about simplification, standardization merits some comment. To standardize something is to use the same words every time. For ex-

ample, performers are not served well when they are told to "Press Enter" many different ways ("Depress," "Strike," "Hit," "Tap on," and so on). When performers see the same phrase every time, they begin to read the phrase in the same way they would a single word. Hence they read with greater ease, speed, and comprehension.

3. How can I make it active, personal, and present? Use active voice rather than passive. Passive voice is more difficult to understand than active, direct sentences. Passive voice construction reduces reading speed by up to 25 percent. However, passive voice can sometimes serve a purpose. For example, you may use it occasionally to emphasize what is done rather than who is doing it. But make passive voice sentences the exception rather than the rule, and never use passive voice when you can use active.

Weak Sentence Constructions
The following password should be entered.
The engineer should carefully review her data before proceeding.

Better Sentence Constructions
Enter the following password.
Carefully review your data before proceeding.

Write in second person; use direct address when possible. As a general rule, write as if you are speaking directly to the performers. Studies show that performers tend to slip into the less involved role of observers when addressed in third person. They adopt a much more active role when addressed directly through the use of second person. (Note, however, that if a job aid has several potential audiences, second person may cause confusion unless you make it very clear who is being addressed. Also, if you are describing negative behavior, third person can be less threatening to readers.)

Weak Sentence Construction
The user should take care and follow directions in using his or her workstation.

Better Sentence Construction
Take care and follow directions in using your workstation.

Write in present tense. However, there are situations in which it is appropriate to use past or future tense. Past tense may be used to present occasional historical information, such as case histories. Future tense should be used to describe predicted actions.

Present Tense
Highlight the option you want by using the up and down arrow keys.

Past Tense
If the desired information does not appear on the screen, the original data was not entered correctly.

Future Tense
In this video burst, you will learn the following skills.

Use Typography to Enhance Readability

Proper application of the principles of good typography can increase the readability of a job aid. Reading speed is directly affected by the type and style of fonts used, the length of lines, and the space between those lines (leading). In addition, typography choices can hinder or help the performers' search for information. When making typography decisions, use common sense. Just because you have the ability to use many different types of fonts, don't. Keep things simple, and use only a few. Even though the absence or presence of white space does not hinder or help readability, the fact that people prefer white space should influence you to use it. And realize that readers need sufficient contrast between the color of the background and the text. For example, gray text on a gray background can create a readability threat. To use typography to improve readability, consider following these general guidelines:

1. Use boldface type for emphasis. Boldface type will not slow a

user's reading rate. Avoid using boldface type for blocks of text longer than two lines.

2. Consider using ragged-right margins when text extends across most of the page or screen, the font size is small, and/or the leading is tight.

3. Do not use all uppercase letters for body text or lines where you want performers to scan quickly (for example, headings or reference statements). The lowercase letters have ascenders and descenders (see Figure 4.2). These parts of letters that stick up above and down below the body of words provide visual cues that allow the eye to recognize the words more rapidly than when they are stripped from the word pattern by using all uppercase text.

4. Vary leading (the space between lines) according to the selected line length and typeface. Typefaces with longer ascenders and descenders and also with a large X height require more leading. Serif type requires less leading than sans serif. (Serifs are the extensions on the ends of letters. A sans serif font lacks these extensions)

5. Avoid using italics for entire sentences or paragraphs.

6. Keep the line length to less than 2.5 alphabets (65 characters).

7. Avoid multilevel numbering of text headings (for example, 4.3.1). Show the relationships of information visually instead.

8. When possible, limit the number of heading levels to three.

9. Use serif fonts that are nondecorative for large bodies of text. Serifs help contribute to unique word patterns that facilitate more rapid recognition of those words. As a result, most people read faster with greater ease and comprehension. But, when visual conditions are poor due to dimmed lighting or increased distance between performers and the text they need to read, use sans serif fonts instead. They are more legible (recognizable).

Examples of decorative fonts are shown in Figure 4.3.

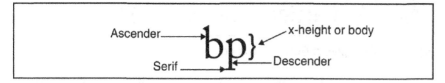

Figure 4.2. Ascender and Descender on a Lowercase Letter

Establish Proper Graphic Conventions

Graphics can facilitate the usability of most job aids. But don't assume that visuals are easier to interpret than written text. This is not always the case. Visual literacy is an acquired skill. Just as you have learned to read, you have also learned to interpret visuals.

In technical settings especially, readers are confronted with graphic conventions that are not common to previous experience. This can easily cause misunderstandings. To avoid this, you should always provide a key that defines the visual conventions you use.

Conventions should also be applied consistently across all your Performance Support solutions. Inconsistency creates an underlying confusion. As you establish proper graphic conventions, consider following these general guidelines:

1. Define all graphic conventions.
2. Use icons and other graphic conventions sparingly and consistently.
3. Keep visuals simple, and limit visual noise.
4. If a visual consists of new or unfamiliar symbols, define them.
5. Use graphics:
    o When a literal example is warranted (for example, a computer screen or piece of equipment)
    o To convey complex defined concepts (for example, visual analogies such as the image of an air traffic control tower to convey the concept of how a data router works)
    o As a cueing device (icons)

Curley, **Ar Cartier,** *AR Decode,* AR Herman

Figure 4.3. Examples of Decorative Fonts

> o To provide feedback or convey successful completion of an action where there is a visual result (for example, part of a report that is produced as the end result of a task)

Guidelines for Designing Planners

The first step in designing a planner is to determine if a planner is needed. Table 4.2 can help you make that decision. And if a planner is needed, it will help you determine which of the moments of need you should design your planner to support. In addition, the right-hand column provides a listing of design guidelines. See www .mhprofessional.com/InnovativePerformanceSuppport for examples of planner job aids.

Guidelines for Designing Sidekicks

The first step in designing a sidekick is to determine if a sidekick is needed. Table 4.3 can help you make that decision. And if a sidekick is needed, it will help you determine which of the moments of need you should design your sidekick to support. In addition, the right-hand column provides a listing of design guidelines. See http://per formersupport.ning.com for examples of sidekick job aids.

Guidelines for Designing Task-Based Sidekicks (System, Nonsystem, Principle Governed)

There are three types of task-based sidekicks: system, nonsystem, and principle governed. System task sidekicks support performers

Table 4.2. Some of the Questions to Answer in Designing a Planner

Moment of Need	Is There a Need for Support before Performance? (Planners)	
Apply	Do performers need help remembering specific tasks prior to performing those tasks?	• Provide access to task sidekicks. • Tie task sidekicks to accelerated demonstrations. • Consider concept learning bursts. • To facilitate retrieval, use encoding models that have been used previously.
	Do performers need to review specific concepts prior to performing related tasks?	• Anticipate and provide for multiple access options based on job roles and work requirements. • Provide contextual access via workflow. • Employ, when possible, parametric search capability. • Automate key search options.
	Is there information performers need to review prior to performance? Would a planning tool be useful?	A planning tool may be a checklist that performers can follow to help them consider every planning option. It might be a form that they complete or a data manipulation tool with which performers input data and the tool manipulates that data into a form that will contribute to successful performance.
Change	Have there been changes in performance requirements that require planning prior to performing? Is there a significant amount of new or updated information that requires mental processing prior to acting upon it?	• Provide an impact rating of each change item along with a recommended "performance change" path that performers can use to plan how they will unlearn and relearn. • Provide immediate access to the new or updated information. Make sure the changes are highlighted with ties to the job and organizational impact ratings.

(continued)

Solve	Are there potential problems and/ or challenges that require planning?	Note: See the discussion of troubleshooting guidelines later in the chapter for elaboration on the following five guidelines. • Identify the most common questions and/or challenges that performers face for a specific performance area. Provide an explanation with a solution. • Provide decision trees. • Provide troubleshooting tips. • Provide links to troubleshooting concepts. • Define an overarching troubleshooting process for a specific performance area.
Learn New	Will there be performers who haven't participated in formal training in this area who need to learn a skill that requires planning? Should lessons learned be available as planners?	Note: See "Guidelines for Designing Learning Bursts" later in the chapter for elaboration on the following six guidelines. • Keep learning bursts short, focused, and engaging. • Provide context maps. • Provide visual support. • Avoid visual noise. • Consider visual analogies. • Blend in application tools When the consequences of failure are great, access to lessons learned becomes a vital resource to performers by way of planners.
Learn More	Will there be performers who need additional training in this area for a skill that requires planning?	Note: See "Guidelines for Designing Learning Bursts" later in the chapter.

in using software and/or hardware devices in their workflow process. Nonsystem task sidekicks support performance tasks that are manual in nature and that are essentially clear, straightforward procedures unrelated to technology (for example, changing a part of a motor or assembling a piece of equipment). A governing principle is a guiding generalization that can be used as a basis for reasoning or conduct. For example, when confronted by an irate customer, a

Table 4.3. Some of the Questions to Answer in Designing a Sidekick

Moment of Need	Is There a Need for Support during Performance? (Sidekicks)	
Apply	Do performers need help remembering and/or completing specific tasks (system, nonsystem, principle governed)? Are there tasks or principles that independently merit real-time support? Do performers need access to information? Do performers need access to specific tools?	• If yes, see the guidelines for designing task-based sidekicks later in the chapter. • Infrequently completed tasks generally aren't internalized even though they were part of the formal training curriculum. As a result, they merit being supported with a sidekick. Not only do task-based sidekicks support remembering but they can also help performers complete tasks that were never introduced during training. • Whenever the consequences of failure are high, a sidekick is justified. • Often, Performance Support doesn't require supporting the steps of doing something. Rather, it calls for providing instantaneous and intuitive access to the information that performers need during the performance (for example, specific customer information, specific product information). • Often, organizations develop tools that performers need to access in the flow of their work that help them complete their work (for example, checklists, templates, and data calculators). Providing access to these tools at the moment of need is a role that Performance Support should play.
Change	Has there been any change in performance requirements? Is there new or updated information?	• Both of these situations call for a Performance Support solution employing sidekicks.
Solve	Are there potential problems and/or challenges?	• If yes, see the guidelines for designing job aids for troubleshooting later in this chapter.

(continued)

Learn New	Will there be performers who haven't participated in formal training in this area?	• If yes, see the guidelines for designing learning bursts later in this chapter.
Learn More	Do aspects of the performance requirements call for additional training?	• If yes, see the guidelines for designing learning bursts later in this chapter.

sales representative might employ the principle of "empathy" and "sincere compliments" to help soften the customer's attitude. The use of these guiding principles doesn't guarantee the customer will alter his mood, but generally it will. A principle-governed task-based sidekick has steps that include guiding principles. For example, if the first step in a task is "Greet the customer," the sidekick might also include reference to guiding principles such as "Convey personal warmth and interest."

The list below provides some overarching guidelines, which are followed by specific guidelines for these three types of task-based sidekicks.

Overarching Guidelines for Task-Based Sidekicks

- Convey the purpose of the sidekick. This can often be accomplished by the labels you use.
  - o Use action labels. When performers look at a label, they need to determine by that label what it is they are going to do. It doesn't take much to accomplish this. When you use verb labels (for example, "Create a new document") consistently to represent tasks rather than noun labels (for example, "Document creation"), performers will intuitively recognize the purpose of the sidekick.
  - o Use performer-focused language. The language you use for labels needs to reflect the performance culture

of your audiences. Don't become so close to the subject matter that you forget that performers may lack the same familiarity. For example, instead of the label "Complete the PF4.09 screen," you might use the label "Enter a patient's billing information." Or instead of the label "Use the electronic clipboard," you might consider a less technical one like "Cut and paste information." Or if your audience wouldn't understand the label "cut and paste," you might say, "Move selected information from place to place." Again, the intent of this guideline is that you use language that will be most familiar to your audiences, language that reflects that business environment and culture.

- Link to roles and workflow process.
  - o The guidelines for workflow, introduced in the previous chapter, apply here.
  - o Use the same visual context maps introduced in training. This will help facilitate retrieval of what performers learned and reinforce it as they use the sidekick.
- Provide a key for any graphic conventions.
  - o See the general guidelines for graphics presented earlier in this chapter.
- Adapt the sidekicks to accommodate the nature of the tasks and the performer community whom you are supporting. For example, procedures having serious consequences should be described in greater detail than procedures that do not. Also, the sidekicks you create for audiences who are "transforming" in nature can be more abbreviated than those you create for "conforming" audiences. Transforming audiences are individuals who are self-directed and independent. Conforming audiences are dependent learners who require structured learning approaches.
- Provide an overview when the underlying content for the sidekick is lengthy.

- Provide multiple access options.
  - o See the guidelines in the Conduct an Access Analysis section in the next chapter.

Specific Guidelines for Designing System-Related Sidekicks

Include only those types of sidekicks that are relevant to the kind of application you are supporting (see Table 4.4). The type of sidekick that is the best one to use will differ according to the nature of the software. Software driven by menus, function keys, and icons can be summarized by a procedure path sidekick. A command table provides an overview for software that is governed mostly by commands. Software that contains screens requires two types of sidekicks: a screen overview and a fields overview. When procedures contain multiple screens but the fields for each screen are unique, a screen sidekick is appropriate. If there is significant overlap of fields from screen to screen, a fields sidekick works best.

The general guidelines and specific standards given in Table 4.4 will help you create the appropriate blend of system task-based sidekicks. Consider the types of sidekicks described, and use the ones that work best with your software.

Specific Guidelines for Designing Principle-Governed Sidekicks

A principle-based sidekick functions the same way as a system-related task sidekick. The only differences are that the application of a principle doesn't guarantee a consistent result and often the sequence of actions isn't clear. For example, a call center has a process called "Finalize the sale," and one of the tasks is "Respond to objections." To accomplish this task, there is a series of principle-based steps the operator would follow, such as the steps shown in Figure 4.4. As you can see, these steps may or may not bring about the desired result of overcoming an objection. Although there is a somewhat logical sequential order to the steps in this task, the performer could opt to modify the sequence based on specific circumstances.

Often, principle-governed tasks are intermixed with system and nonsystem tasks. See, for example, Table 4.5.

Table 4.4. Guidelines and Specific Standards for Sidekicks

Icons	Create an *icon sidekick* whenever an application uses icons as a graphic interface (for example, using icons to represent different file types). Each icon should be listed in the glossary along with a definition of its purpose with references to where it is discussed in greater detail.
Commands	A *command sidekick* provides a functional and alphabetical listing of all commands. The nature of a command sidekick varies depending upon the number and complexity of the commands. The sidekick can be as simple as a table listing each command with a brief description, an example, and references to where the command is discussed in greater detail. When the commands are complex in nature (for example, commands written in job control language), the sidekick can contain a full-page-length description for each command. This command summary page lists the command syntax, provides a complex and simple example of the command, describes the purpose and use of the command, and defines all required and optional parameters. Obviously this sidekick would be best delivered digitally with multiple access options including search.
	A *command key sidekick* is helpful when an application employs command keys ([Ctrl]), (1, [Shift]) alone or in concert with other keys, menu selections, and screens to accomplish specific tasks. This sidekick would be accessed functionally and/or alphabetically. In either case, consider a table listing each function followed by the procedure path. The procedure path would list, in order, the keys, menu selections, and information to be entered. The following example illustrates the procedure path for creating (inserting) a ruler: [F1] 3 I (Set ruler) (Return).
Menus	A *menu sidekick* shows the entire menu structure of an application. This can be accomplished with menu trees or menu outlines. A menu tree graphically shows all menu relationships. A menu outline is a list or table that includes a brief statement of purpose.
Tasks	A *task sidekick* provides superquick, step-by-step instructions for completing specific tasks. These references are *quick-path reminders* of how to perform a task. Here are some specific guidelines for this type of sidekick:
	1. For software, a digital sidekick is preferable as long as there is sufficient screen size and the sidekick can remain ever present while the performer is working within the application.
	2. Whenever possible, provide deeper support to the quick path with the ability of the performers to access more detailed information if needed (including simulations or emerging software agents that guide performers, in real time, through each task while they are literally working within the application).

(continued)

Tasks *(continued)*	3. Don't document every possible approach. Often multiple methods exist to accomplish a single task. Menu-driven applications may have a common procedure where the only variation is the menu selection (for example, printing various reports). Command-driven applications may present commands that have optional parameters and variables that result in too many options to cover in one document. In these instances, what you want to achieve is a generalized skill. For example, if the sidekick is needed to support "Printing reports," and the reports are generated from a common menu, you would write the step-by-step instructions for printing a generic report highlighting where the decision points are for producing different reports. 4. Visually separate input from output. 5. Include a rationale for each step. Write the comments you would make if sitting at the user's side. These comments can include information such as the following: • Explanatory comments • References to related concepts • Descriptions of possible error messages with solutions • Examples Depending on the experience level of your audiences and the amount of rationale, you may opt to include the rationale as part of the more detailed option. 6. Standardize your use of the command verbs. For example:

Select	Use when choosing an option from a menu. (Select Properties from the File menu.).
Press	Use when pressing keys on the keyboard. (Press F8 for another view.)
Highlight	Use when clicking on a word or icon in preparation to drag or right click with the mouse. (Highlight the Recycle bin, and drag it to the left of your desktop.)
Click on	Use when instructing the performer to use the mouse. Whether it's a standard click or a right click, the word *on* should follow. (Click on File.)
Drag	Use after the word *highlight* when an item or icon is being moved. (Highlight the Recycle bin and drag it to the left of your desktop.)
Enter	Use only when referring to the Enter button on the keyboard. (Press Enter to continue to the next menu.)
Double click	Use whenever the user needs to double click the mouse button.
Type	Use when entering information. (Type the relevant information in the Personal Information section.)
Choose	Use when there are more two or more options for completing a step. (Choose a method to save your work.)

Tasks
(continued)
	7. When there are multiple methods to accomplish a task, select and document the most safe and most common method.
	8. Separate actual input from all other text. For example:
	
	Step 4. To rename the file, type:
	rename sys txt all together
	and press Enter.
	
	9. Distinguish actions that put a user at risk (Warning) and actions that could cause damage to equipment or data (Caution).
	10. Nest simple, related steps together into a *macro step*. For example:
	
	Step 8. In the Receipt Number field:
	    (a) Click on the second receipt row.
	    (b) Click on the New button.
	    (c) Enter the appropriate number.

Screens	Many applications require end users to enter information into several fields on a single screen. A *screen* (or *fields*) *sidekick* provides a summary of these information fields. How you organize this job aid depends on whether the fields are unique to single screens or common across several screens. In the first instance, where fields are unique to specific screens, document the fields by describing entire screens. A *screen summary sidekick* shows the entire screen and defines each field on the screen, with references where the screen is documented in detail. Where fields are common across multiple screens, create a fields sidekick. A *fields sidekick* alphabetically lists every field in a tabular form.
Reports	A *reports sidekick* describes all reports generated by the system and how to access them. Many applications produce reports automatically or on demand. The value of a reports sidekick is that it gives a description of the purpose of each report including who uses it. It also includes sufficient information to facilitate interpretation. This sidekick can be used in at least two ways: 1. Performers can search through the reports to find the procedure they need to follow to print the report. That is, they know how to retrieve the report, but they can't remember how to print it. 2. Once produced, reports deliver value when the right person interprets them and then acts on the conclusions drawn. Sometimes reports are intuitive, and the person studying the report has the inherent capacity to do this. But if this isn't the case, then it is appropriate to include enough explanation to facilitate this within the sidekick. It is often best to have this information as an optional component.

Step 1	Express empathy.
Step 2	Confirm your advocacy.
Step 3	Clarify the issue.
	Turn the issue into a positive.
Step 5	Explore possible workarounds.
Step 6	Seek feedback.

Figure 4.4. A Series of Principle-Based Steps in the Task of Responding to Objections in the Call Center Process for Finalizing a Sale

Here are some guidelines for designing principle-based side-kicks:

1. Whenever possible, express the principles within a task flow tied to a process flow. In Table 4.5, the example of principles for "Respond to objections" is expressed as a task flow. The task flow is part of the process "Finalize the sale." The process "Finalize the sale" is part of a higher-level process: "Selling products and services." See Chapter 3 for discussions regarding the value of linking tasks to a process.

2. Establish a consistent grid. This grid should match the grid you use for system and nonsystem tasks.

3. Whenever possible, provide a quick path with access to more detailed information if needed.

4. Include the rationale for each step. Write the comments you would make if you were sitting at the performer's side. These comments can include the following:

o   Explanatory comments
o   References to related concepts
o   Descriptions of possible error messages with solutions
o   Examples via text, video, and/or audio

Depending on the experience level of your audiences and the amount of rationale you need to include, you may opt to incorporate the rationale as part of the more detailed option.

Table 4.5. A Principle-Based Sidekick for a Call Center Process for Finalizing a Sale

Finalize the Sale		
Task 10	Complete the sale. (System based)	
Task 11	Respond to objections. (Principle based)	
Task 12	Ask for referrals. (Principle and system based)	In this task there are several steps where the sales operator enters the referral information into the system.
Task 13	Schedule a follow-up. (Principle and system-based)	Follow-up dates are entered into the system.
Task 14	Recap and close. (Principle based)	

Guidelines for Designing Quick-Checks

In the discipline of instructional and learning design, we most often view evaluation as something we do to determine if performers achieved what we set out to help them achieve. We measure the merit and worth of the experience. We work to deduce the return on investment as a result. This is all fine and good, but evaluation has much more to offer. Evaluation can and should be a principle of instruction, not just a phase in the training development process. When we train people how to evaluate their own performance, we place them on a path of ongoing improvement. When we provide them tools to ensure that their self-evaluation is objective and deliberate, we ensure that ongoing growth occurs at maximum potential.

Quick-checks help performers review their performance, determine how they could have performed better, and take the steps necessary to perform better next time they are called upon to act in a similar manner.

Michael J. Gelb wrote, "Champions know that success is inevitable, that there is no such thing as failure, only feedback."[1] Self-evaluation can be the most influential form of feedback possible. It ensures persistent growth. It may very well be the most powerful principle of instruction and learning. And it certainly has a vital role to play in performer support.

Here are some guidelines to help you develop and implement quick-checks.

Develop Self-Assessment Tools, and Then Bring Those Tools into Formal Training

As we have recommended with all other performer support tools, a fundamental objective in formal training is to train performers how to use their performer support tools. This should especially include learning how to use the self-evaluation tools you create. People aren't naturally objective in how they view their own performance. They are often too harsh or too soft in their assessments. There is mighty instructional power in engaging performers in the process of evaluation of each other's performance as well as their own. Here's how you can go about it:

- Begin by having students evaluate the performance of other people they don't know. Use this opportunity to help them hone their skills in recognizing performance levels that are less than desirable.

- Transition to peer evaluation coupled with self-evaluation. These evaluation teams should be large enough to ensure that objective evaluation takes place. Where there are discrepancies, have the team members work to resolve those differences.

Provide Capability for Ongoing Capture of and Access to Lessons Learned

When the performance landscape is challenging and changing, there is value in providing people the ability to capture the lessons they are learning along the way so they can draw upon them when needed. And if the consequences of failure merit it, these best-practice solutions should be gathered in a manner that will allow them to be shared with others who face the same or similar sets of performance challenges. Table 4.6 provides sample questions to do so.

Guidelines for Designing Job Aids for Troubleshooting

The moment of Solve requires job aids that support the skill of troubleshooting. Often these PS tools need to help performers diagnose the cause of a problem and ascertain the solution. The following guidelines illustrate some ways for doing this.

1. Identify the most common questions and/or challenges that performers face in a specific performance area. Provide an explanation with a solution. Table 4.7 provides some examples.

Provide Decision Trees

These job aids are helpful when there is a clear diagnostic path. These trees should have a main trunk (in Table 4.8, the trunk is the left column.). The branches to the right should either end or

Table 4.6. Some of the Questions to Answer in Capturing and Providing Access to Lessons Learned

Moment of Need	Is There a Need for Support after Performance? (Quick-Checks)	
Apply	Is there justification for individual pursuit of ongoing performance improvement?	Some skills such as tasks for which there are discrete sets of steps with minimal qualitative requirements do not merit this pursuit. However, principle-based skills such as interpersonal skills have high qualitative requirements, and therefore they most likely merit this pursuit.
	Is there opportunity for peer evaluation?	Peer evaluation is an effective transition practice for helping performers develop their self-assessment skills. A yes here strengthens the case for quick-checks but doesn't preclude them.
	Is there a need to capture lessons learned in support of Apply?	There is a need when the nature of performance is qualitative. This can be a vital contributor to ongoing performance improvement.
	Is there capability to capture performance for postevaluation?	Some skills are more measurable than others—especially by performers themselves. An example is when performance produces outcomes that can be reviewed and therefore assessed or when performance is recorded for postviewing. More difficult is evaluating real-time performance that fails to produce any tangible outcomes.
Change	Should performers determine their own personal performance gaps?	This is a critical postperformance capability particularly in an environment where change is constant. If performers need to be adaptive in their work, the goal of Performance Support should include helping performers determine their own personal performance gaps.
Solve	Is the determination of the problem resolution counterintuitive?	Obviously if the resolution of problems is counterintuitive, there is a need to provide some sort of help. The point here is that there are often problems that have intuitive resolution paths. These don't merit the same Performance Support investment at the moment of Solve.
	Is there ongoing value in capturing solutions with lessons learned?	To the degree that others are able to perform effectively in less time and/or with fewer resource requirements, there is justification in capturing solutions with lessons learned.

Learn New	Are there learning outcomes that merit the investment in performance assessment?	When there are performance outcomes that contribute to the bottom line of an organization's well-being, there is merit in investing in performance assessment, especially self-assessment.
Learn More	Are there ongoing learning outcomes that merit the investment in performance assessment?	Same as above.

Table 4.7. Common Questions and Challenges Performers Face in Specific Performance Areas

Question or Issue	Solution	Explanation
Last names with titles (for example, Jr., Sr.), when they follow the first names, do not sort correctly.	To solve this problem, a *hard space* must be inserted between the last name and the title so that both words sort as only one word.	A *hard space* code allows the software to recognize two words as one while displaying them as two separate words. This feature can also be used to keep two or more words together on the same line. When you put a *hard space* between two words, the system will either fit the words on the current line or wrap them both to the following line.
Error Message	**Explanation**	**Solution**
Packed file is corrupt.	This message displays if a portion of memory that is inaccessible has been encountered or general problems with installation of the program files are has occurred.	Reinstall the program from the master disk. Download the file TESTMEM}COM. (This file is designed to test the system's memory.) Many times the order in which the internal memory chips were installed is the problem. The largest memory chip on the controller board should be positioned last.

branch back into the trunk. In the following job aid, all branches to the right end the diagnostic process except for step 2, which has a branching option back to the trunk.

Obviously there are many ways to graphically represent a decision tree. More traditional flowcharts may be needed if there is branching away from the trunk. The example in Figure 4.5 was developed by PS community member Leroy Dennison.

Provide Troubleshooting Tips

A job aid is helpful when there isn't a clear diagnostic path but there are tips that may help resolve or prevent a problem. Table 4.9 illustrates a job aid for troubleshooting tips.

Table 4.8. An Example of a Decision Tree

	Problem: Document Is Not Printing		
1	Is there a message in printer control?	Yes	Refer to the *error message solutions* job aid.
	No		
2	Is the power on? Is the printer online? Are the cables tight?	No	Take appropriate action.
			Still not working? Go to step 3.
	Yes		
3	Is the printer setup (definition, port, and so on) correct in the software?		
	Download and run: systemcheck.exe	No	Select: Correct Setup, and at Done, press Return, Return.
	Yes		
4	Is document printing?	No	Call the Technical Assistance Center (TAC).

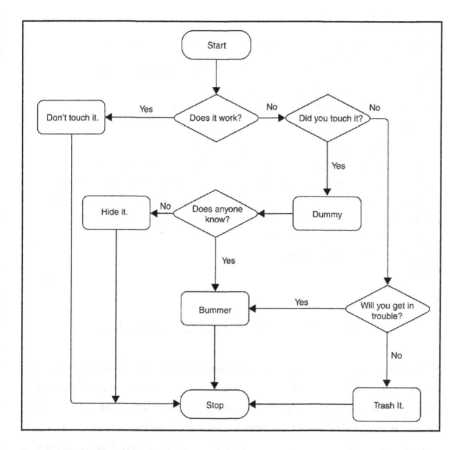

Figure 4.5. An Example of a Decision Tree
Source: Leroy Dennison.

Provide Links to Troubleshooting Concepts

Sometimes, problems can be solved by tying back to concepts previously learned or that need to be learned at the moment of Solve. Figure 4.6 is an example of the troubleshooting concept. The example was developed by Mary Ortiz [Training Coordinator Holcim (U.S.), Inc., 6211 Ann Arbor Road, Dundee, Michigan, e-mail Mary.Ortiz@ holcim.com].

Table 4.9. An Example of Job Aid Troubleshooting Tips

	Common Causes of Macro Problems	Macro Tips to Remember
Troubleshooting Macros	• A large majority of macro problems are due to missing tildes at the end of a command. (A tilde is a delimiter.) • Many problems are directly related to commands in the macro that do not make sense or are not possible in the program. These problems are usually caused when you are trying to create a macro from your own memory (with Display off).	• Always keep Display on when creating or testing a macro. This allows you to see the contents of the macro as it runs. • The Speed command can be used to slow down the macro when testing, making it easier to follow the logic of the macro.

Guidelines for Designing Learning Bursts

A *learning burst* is a short training segment that focuses on a single concept or task. It can be combined with other bursts to become a complete learning module. Learning bursts can exist in different form factors: e-learning (Internet, mobile), video, audio, recorded virtual instructor-led training (VILT), and annotated simulations.

Learning bursts support performers at the moment of Apply when they need to learn something New or learn More, or in some cases to remember. Here's an example of how a learning burst can deliver support. A regional sales leader has responsibility for a force that is struggling in their sales performance. To increase sales, the manager provides the team access to 100 video learning bursts, each lasting three to seven minutes. These bursts are divided into different series teaching fundamental skill sets that support the selling process. The sales team can access these bursts via the Internet through their mobile devices and workstations. Each series (five to nine bursts) has a *digital planning agent* that the sales representatives can use to bring in specific client data to populate an agenda and a *slide deck* to use during the client's visit. The planning agent also

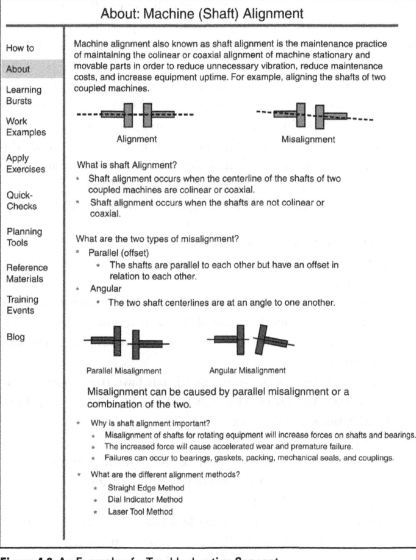

About: Machine (Shaft) Alignment

How to

About

Learning Bursts

Work Examples

Apply Exercises

Quick-Checks

Planning Tools

Reference Materials

Training Events

Blog

Machine alignment also known as shaft alignment is the maintenance practice of maintaining the colinear or coaxial alignment of machine stationary and movable parts in order to reduce unnecessary vibration, reduce maintenance costs, and increase equipment uptime. For example, aligning the shafts of two coupled machines.

Alignment   Misalignment

What is shaft Alignment?
* Shaft alignment occurs when the centerline of the shafts of two coupled machines are colinear or coaxial.
* Shaft alignment occurs when the shafts are not colinear or coaxial.

What are the two types of misalignment?
* Parallel (offset)
    * The shafts are parallel to each other but have an offset in relation to each other.
* Angular
    * The two shaft centerlines are at an angle to one another.

Parallel Misalignment   Angular Misalignment

Misalignment can be caused by parallel misalignment or a combination of the two.

* Why is shaft alignment important?
    * Misalignment of shafts for rotating equipment will increase forces on shafts and bearings.
    * The increased force will cause accelerated wear and premature failure.
    * Failures can occur to bearings, gaskets, packing, mechanical seals, and couplings.
* What are the different alignment methods?
    * Straight Edge Method
    * Dial Indicator Method
    * Laser Tool Method

Figure 4.6. An Example of a Troubleshooting Concept
Source: Mary Ortiz

generates a client-specific digital checklist and pushes it to the sales team member's mobile device.

The sales manager uses virtual classroom technology to train the sales team in how to use the planning agent and provide them an overview to the learning burst series. Each day the sales manager pushes a video burst out to the sales team to view as they begin their day with the challenge to apply the principles presented in the burst throughout that day and to complete the digital checklist (quick-check) after each client visit.

Individual sales agents can also access any of the other 100 bursts if they determine they need to learn a skill needed for a specific sales call. They can view the burst just prior to stepping into a call. In this case, the agent would be using the learning burst to support the agents' learning at the moment of New or More, and it would occur prior to the moment of Apply so it would be a planner.

Here are some guidelines for designing learning bursts:

1. Keep them short, focused, and engaging. They should be three to seven minutes long and restricted to a single task, concept, or example.
2. Provide context maps. Learning bursts need to weave together to facilitate the development of skill sets. It is helpful to provide context maps that show how a specific learning burst fits into the larger picture.
3. Use visuals to support learning. Visuals have the capacity to be more than decorative. They can facilitate learning. See Dr. Ruth Clark's book entitled *Graphics for Learning: Proven Guidelines for Planning, Designing, and Evaluating Visuals in Training Materials* for more information about the use of visuals to support learning.
4. Tie them to job aids. PS tools are particularly critical here. Learning bursts often lack the innate capacity to facilitate the transition to performance. For example, a video learning burst can be engaging and informative but also weak when it comes to Apply. Application tools can also be helpful here such as digital games and simulations.

Guidelines for Making Reference Information Accessible

There are times when the moment of Apply doesn't require a planner, sidekick, or quick-check. All that is needed to ensure effective performance is access to the right information. In these instances, performers have the skills, but the information required to complete the task has changed or was never internalized because it is always changing, too vast, or infrequently needed. Whatever the reason, many times performance needs information that the performers lack. In these instances the PS strategy needs to provide intuitive access to the right content in the right form.

1. Anticipate and provide for multiple access options based upon job roles and work requirements. Search covers a multitude of weaknesses in a Performance Support strategy. The challenge of search is that it often yields too many hits. Searching through search results can be costly for organizations. Certainly narrowing accessible content by job role can help reduce the number of hits search delivers; however, there is another option that can prove effective. Here's what you do:

    Step 1. For every type of content (for example, task, concept, or business policy), identify all the access options. For example, if the content type were recipes, performers might want to access them by occasion, primary ingredient, preparation time, dietary requirement, course, and so on.

    Step 2. Narrow the access options to those that would be of highest use to your audiences, and build those access options into your content management system.

2. Push for parametric search. Some search engines employ parametric search to narrow the search based upon parameters like job role, work group, type of information (for example, task, concept, or report), or unique access option. For example, if the type of information were "reports," the options might be by date or by data source. All these parameters are attached to the content as metadata tags, and it takes very few of the parameters to drill into a specific instance of needed information.

3. Provide contextual access via workflow. The previous chapter focused on this critical principle.

HOW YOU CAN APPLY THIS

This chapter has focused on many design principles. These principles and the content they support require a *means of delivery*. These *deliverables* have strengths and limitations. The best practices are that you use them according to their strengths and you be careful about the weaknesses. The following analysis will help you do this.

Conduct a Deliverables Analysis

We recall an organization that was implementing a digital Performance Support system to support employees at the cash register. The digital PS system was loaded on a lonely PC located in the employee break room. There was no access at the cash registers. The PS system was well designed. The company had followed many of the principles presented in this chapter. But it did very little good. The company had chosen the wrong deliverable for the content.

Deliverables analysis is a procedure that can help you select the most appropriate deliverables to support performance at the moment of Apply. The core performer support deliverables are these:

- Paper-based job aids
- Electronic (digital) job aids
- Web reference content
- Mobile Performance Support
- Learning bursts
- Brokers

To conduct a deliverables analysis, do the following:

Step 1. Complete the checklist in Table 4.10.
Step 2. Check your assessment by having at least one other person independently complete the checklist.
Step 3. Resolve any discrepancies between the checklist responses.

Table 4.10. A Checklist for Conducting a Deliverables Analysis

1			
		Are Paper-Based Job Aids Workable Options?	
Y	**N**	**Issue**	**Comments**
		Is the content stable?	Unstable content requires continuous updating. Depending on the rate of change, trying to maintain current content in paper-based job aids can be costly. Performers falter with inaccurate information, and those charged with maintaining the job aids become consumed in a maintenance nightmare. If the content is unstable, then consider a different deliverable.
		Is there a single level of content structure?	Paper-based job aids work very well when there is only one to two levels of content. You can efficiently produce a paper-based job aid under these circumstances. But when there are three or more levels, it becomes difficult to help performers navigate through those levels and keep them straight in a paper-based job aid. So if this is the case, then consider a different deliverable.
		Is digital delivery an unworkable option (accessibility, reliability)?	There are two threats to digital delivery: accessibility and reliability. Digital delivery requires instantaneous access to technology at the very moment performers are called upon to Apply. If they have to go somewhere or move through a bunch of steps to get to what they need, digital delivery isn't a workable solution. If performers have digital access but the digital solution is unreliable, then performers are potentially left helpless at critical performance times. If either of these comments is true, then digital delivery is unworkable.
		Is there *no* need for performance modeling?	If performers need to see demonstrations of complex human, system, or product performance, then paper-based job aids most likely won't deliver. This is especially the case if audio is needed for the demonstration. In some instances, if the performance is simple and brief, a graphic can show the process (for example, a set of screens showing the sequence of a system task or a line drawing showing the assembly of a product).
If the answer to all of these questions is yes, then paper-based job aids are workable solutions. Keep going though. There may be other deliverables your performers need.			
2			
		To What Degree Should PS Be Electronic (Digital)?	
Y	**N**	**Issue**	**Comments**
		Is performance tied to technology?	This is a no-brainer. If performers are working within a digital environment, then digital Performance Support is the way to go. Probably no need to read through the remaining questions.

(continued)

		Is the content unstable?	Unstable content requires continuous updating. If the content is unstable and if the consequence of performers' acting on inaccurate content is high, then consider a digital PS tool.
		Is the content structure on multiple levels?	This is a sweet spot for digital PS. You can hide levels of content and unveil them when the performers need access to it. When there are three or more levels of content and when the content in the deeper levels is lengthy or extends the detail making it optional to specific needs of performers, digital is the way to go. So if this is the case, then consider it.
		Is digital delivery accessible and reliable?	If performers have intuitive, immediate digital access and the digital solution is reliable, then digital delivery is the way to go.
		Is there a need for performance modeling?	If performers need to see demonstrations of complex human, system, or product performance, then digital is a good solution.

If the answer to these questions is yes, then electronic job aids are workable solutions. Keep going though. There may be other deliverables your performers need.

3			Is There a Need for Web Reference?
Y	N	Issue	Comments
		Does electronic (digital) make sense?	If you answered yes to this in the preceding section, then obviously the answer here is yes.
		Is information reference needed?	If performers need to access information in the context of their performance, then select yes.

If the answer to these two questions is yes, then Web reference is needed. Keep going though. There may be other deliverables your performers need.

4			Is Mobile Support Justifiable?
Y	N	Issue	Comments
		Are performers mobile while needing support?	This is the key reason for mobile support. If people are on the move and need support, there is a good chance that mobile support is justified.

		Do sufficient numbers of performers have access to mobile technology?	If performers are on the move, there is high probability that they have mobile technology, but this nevertheless is a good question to ask.
		Are content requirements deep?	The greater the amount of content and the deeper it is, in terms of levels of information, the greater the need for mobile support.

If the answer to all of these questions is yes, then you should add mobile support to your PS offering. Keep going though. There may be other deliverables your performers need.

5		Are Learning Bursts Needed?	
Y	**N**	**Issue**	**Comments**
		Is there a need to learn New or More at the moment of Apply?	See the discussion on learning bursts earlier in this chapter.

If the answer to this question is yes, then you should add learning bursts to your PS offering. Keep going though. There is high probability you also need a broker.

6		Is There a Need for a Broker?	
Y	**N**	**Issue**	**Comments**
		Do performers need access to content and support tools that reside in different digital locations?	This is one of the fundamental reasons for a broker—it's what brokers do: provide a single-point access to dispersed PS assets.
		Do performers need access to support assets at all five moments of need, before, during, and after the moment of Apply?	This is a second fundamental reason for a broker. If you answer no now, that may not be the case later. The further organizations move down the road of performer support, the greater the probability they will need a broker.
		Does the same content need to be deployed across multiple deliverables?	This is an added function of some broker technologies: *single-source publishing* (SSP). This capability is especially helpful in keeping content current across all the various PS deliverables.

If the answer to all of these questions is yes, then you also need a broker.

INSIGHTS FROM A THOUGHT LEADER: Dr. Allison Rossett

*Allison Rossett is a professor emerita of educational technology at San Diego State University. Dr. Rossett teaches, consults, conducts studies, and presents on topics associated with learning, performance, and technology. She is a member of the HRD Hall of Fame—*Training *magazine's virtual and elite Hall of Fame. She has authored* The ASTD E-learning Handbook: Best Practices, Strategies and Cases, *and she has coauthored* Beyond the Podium: Delivering Training and Performance to a Digital World .

Dr. Rossett was the winner of the International Society for Performance Improvement (ISPI) Instructional Communications award. The following article and model have been adapted from Allison Rossett and Lisa Schafer's book, Job Aids and Performance Support in the Workplace: Moving from Knowledge in the Classroom to Knowledge Everywhere *(Pfeiffer/Wiley, San Francisco, 2007).*

More Performance, Less Training

I think that the most significant thing going on in training and development today is that we have technology, software, and hardware that allow us to punch through the walls of the classroom to deliver expert messages and nudge closer to work. This happens in many ways, via e-coaches, knowledge bases, blogs, wikis, social nets, and Performance Support tools. What all have in common is that they are happening where we work and live. I'd like to focus here on just one form of on-demand delivery: Performance Support.

Performance Support is immediate, targeted, and present. It earns its place by adding value as teachers, doctors, supervisors, seniors, and auditors respond to their tasks and challenges. In these brutal economic times, Performance Support mobilizes messages and thus boosts performance when we can't afford to send an instructor out or bring employees in. Instructors require resources, vacation, and sleep. Performance Support tools do not.

Performance Support Tools

The best way to appreciate Performance Support is to look at examples showing how Performance Support solves problems and elevates practice.

I can remember twiddling my thumbs while waiting to do laundry in my dorm at college. When I wanted to do the wash, the washers and dryers were almost always busy, causing frustration, late nights, and early mornings. When I did get to it, the room, with scattered piles of laundry, wet and dry, disgusted me. This was the result of aggressive launderers who chucked wash on the table if you weren't there to claim it. Enter e-Suds. e-Suds is civilizing the process by introducing information and technology. USA Technologies installed Internet-based laundry systems on several university campuses. The system tracks the use of washers and dryers, and it then alerts students by e-mail, cell, or PDA to the status of their laundry and the washers and dryers in close proximity. Imagine the benefits of knowing the "wash cycle is complete" on your load, or that a washer and dryer is available in Chavez Dormitory, floor 3, north end.

In the first edition of the *Handbook of Job Aids,* Rossett and Gautier-Downes (1991) attempted to expand the ways that people thought about and used job aids. That 1991 enhancement was based on the nature of the content. To traditional job aids that supported information (the Yellow Pages, for example) and procedures (documentation that reminded users how to change the message on an answering machine), Rossett and Gautier-Downes added job aids that coached, advised, and guided decisions. Is this the right graduate school for me? How do I work with an employee who is often tardy? Where should I invest my money, given my circumstances?

While those remain fertile distinctions, what we see today is that effective Performance Support often brings the three together in one computer-based program. For example, a Performance Support program for an individual contemplating graduate education might include a database of possible university programs and prerequisites; procedures for applying; and self-assessment checklists to help potential applicants anticipate readiness and preferences for one program or university over another.

Two dimensions are critical in Performance Support. The first dimension is the degree of integration of the support into the task. Is the Performance Support inside or outside of the task? Is it like your ATM, or is it a computer program that helps you decide how to save for retirement? ATM support is inside, integrated into the task, as you maneuver the screen. The retirement guidelines stand apart; they nudge you to think about this as you consider an investment, answer a question, reflect on a paragraph, and plan for each eventuality, given your situation.

The second dimension for Performance Support is how much tailoring the support offers. Is the support standard for all, or is it actively tailored to your situation? Does it know you and act differently as a result of that knowledge? Consider the difference between support that tells you and every other 55-year-old that you should save for retirement and support that knows you have triplets about to enter college, influential factors in your saving patterns and needs. Is it a mass mailing from your city government about fire danger in California, or a notice sending you to a Web site because the system recognizes that your home is on a canyon, the fire danger is extreme this month, and you must do special kinds of cleanup to mitigate danger?

Integration, Tailoring, and Finding Your Way

Imagine that you have an important appointment across town, at a place you have never been.

Table 4.11 presents alternative support systems to get you to your destination. Focus on the proximity of the support to the challenge.

Table 4.11. Alternative Support Systems for Getting to an Unfamiliar Location

Ways of Getting to an Unfamiliar Destination	Commentary
Consult the city map you have pinned to your wall before you leave.	The map is a job aid, but it is not insinuated into the task, and it is not tailored to you. It doesn't know where you are going or offer guidance on the best way to get there. It will not adapt to your twists and turns or local detours.
Go to MapQuest and enter your address and the destination address. Print the results.	Here we have a conventional print job aid that is insinuated into the task, albeit precariously. As you negotiate the highways and byways, a trusty piece of paper points the way. Note, there is no adaptation to detours or distractions.
Refer to the print results as you drive	Here we see the blending of computer-based performance support and job aids. The online tool is used prior to undertaking the challenge. It is preparation for it.
As you head out the door, ask your brother for directions. He generously provides them.	This may get you there if you have a good memory and your brother is reliable. But insinuated with the task? Definitely not. And when you get distracted and turn left instead of right, his directions will not adjust to your errant ways.
Hop in the car. Dig through the glove box. Pull out a map. Read the map while you drive.	This dangerous job aid is insinuated into the task. It is there as the need to decide RIGHT or LEFT. While integrated into the task, you have to tailor it to you, and at some risk.
Hop in the car and fire up the GPS (Global Positioning System). Key in the destination address. A sultry voice tells you how to get there, no matter where you start or how you diverge.	The GPS support is identified with the task. While there is a display with directions, the directions are little more than comfort because a voice is anticipating what you will need to do and then prompting you to do it. Most interesting is how active the system is, how it adjusts to your location and actions. When you refuse or skip guidance, new advice is calculated for you, tailored to your current location. GPS is both tailored and integrated.

Source: Dr. Allison Rossett.

Let's look at tailoring now. Is the tool offering up a standard, consistent message or one that is customized to your situation? This is a question about the activity level of the tool. Does the tool adjust to you? Does it know you? Does it care which mutual funds you hold, how old you are, how many you must put through college, what products you sell and in which geography, or if you just bypassed the verbal suggestion to turn left at Albatross Street? Does it reach out and nudge and remind about goals? Does it provide a statement of operating procedures or model approaches to customers' objections? The Yellow Pages and Wikipedia are standard, worthy, and passive resources. You go there to find information on Mogadishu or mockingbirds or local veterinarians that specialize in large farm animals. Those trusty resources wait and serve, but they do not customize automatically. You must know what you want and need and go for it. They succeed as support if they house valued resources that are "findable." In our book *Job Aids and Performance Support in the Workplace: Moving from Knowledge in the Classroom to Knowledge Everywhere,* a chapter is devoted to IBM's efforts to make its many substantive resources readily available to far-flung employees.

Schwab.com and Quitnet.com are different in that their Performance Support is actively targeted to you. They know you and your goals—and your circumstances. Schwab will help you reach financial goals. Quitnet is there to help the individual who wants to stop smoking turn away from a cigarette after a long, hard day at work. Both tailor responses based on answers you provide to them and "know" you when you return to the site for advice because you are craving a cigarette or trying to decide where to invest a royalty check. The knowledge goes where the need is, when it presents itself.

Introducing Planners and Sidekicks

Performance Support is an information-rich asset that a nurse, teacher, parent, mechanic, taxpayer, pilot, or auditor turns to for help in getting things done. Performance Support appears in many forms, from notes on matchbook covers to well-worn documentation, to posters to ehelp.com, financial planning tools, and GPS. Because there are so many possibilities, Lisa Schafer and I, in *Job Aids and Performance Support in the Workplace: Moving from Knowledge in the Classroom to Knowledge Everywhere,* tamed the domain into two kinds of Performance Support: planners and sidekicks.

Planners are in our lives just before or after the challenge. They help us decide if Avian Flu or piracy at sea should alter our trip plans. I use one to help me think hard and comprehensively as I tailor a presentation for a group.

Sidekicks are at our side during the task. The quick food cook reads the job aid as she creates the new food product. The quarterback glances at his wrist in the huddle. The writer pecks

Table 4.12. Using Performance Support to Assist with a Sale

Performance Support	Standard	Tailored
Sidekicks: They are with us in the work, as we act.	Here the customer and salesperson look at a PC and examine a table that compares the recommended product to its competitors	When the customer picks a product configuration, the salesperson identifies the customer, and the system details what it will take to achieve compatibility with this customer's current installed base.
Planners: They are there when we get ready to act and afterwards, when we reflect on our efforts.	This is a print or automated program that reminds a salesperson what to keep in mind when selling at higher levels in the organization. Afterwards, the salesperson can reflect on the interaction in light of the criteria.	This is an automated program that seeks data about a potential customer, qualifies the customer, and then informs the salesperson of the size loan for which he or she will qualify. The amount and rationale are provided to the salesperson to aid in countering objections.

Source: Dr. Allison Rossett.

away and smiles at how wikis once earned a red line under it in this sentence, but no longer does. Sidekicks vary in how close they are to the task. They might be next to the task, as is the case with the cook and quarterback, or integrated into the thick of it, as in the spelling checker.

Now let us add the question of customization. Is it guidance for everybody interested in the product or hurricanes or retirement, or does it know you and your situation and tailor advice accordingly? Table 4.12 illustrates the model applied to sales.

Performance Matters

Planners and sidekicks have a long history and a bright future as we lean on Performance Support to improve interactions, spell correctly, satisfy customers, stock the house for nutritious eating, and make smart and fair decisions about whom to hire. It makes sense to move from knowledge in the classroom to knowledge everywhere, since that is where life and work happen . . . everywhere

5

BROKERING
YOUR LEARNING ASSETS

Most of us feel overburdened by information, although I would say the overloaded feeling comes more from coordinating all of the information and responding to it.

—*Dave Rose*

A STORY TO GET STARTED: THE STREET LIGHT INCIDENT

There once was a man who was approaching his parked car after a night out on the town. He suddenly realized he had lost his car keys. He frantically began crawling along the ground looking for his keys. A passerby, seeing the situation that the poor gentleman was in, asked if he could help. The forlorn driver immediately accepted his offer, and the two began searching together.

After several minutes of not finding the keys, the Good Samaritan asked, "So where do you remember last seeing them?"

To which the driver responded, "Over by my car parked around the corner."

The other gentleman immediately rolled his eyes in disgust after all this time of searching and said, "Well, why aren't we looking over there?"

"Because the light's so much better over here," the man replied while pointing to the streetlight beaming overhead.

Have you ever found this to be the case when attempting to find the correct learning asset from the many that exist throughout your organization? Many of the companies we've helped in moving their learning to the moment of Apply have shared that the problem isn't the lack of Performance Support assets. It's the inability to find the right one at the right time. This chapter will focus on the critical concept of *Performance Support brokers*, the keys to solving this all-too-common problem.

Read on if you want to learn how to accomplish this by effectively brokering learning assets at the moment of Apply. And if you want to see an example of a broker, see www.mhprofessional.com/Inno vativePerformanceSuppport.

WHAT YOU NEED TO KNOW

In the early 1990s many in the learning industry believed that e-learning would become the next Performance Support platform. Because it was delivered directly to the performers' desktops when they wanted it, we assumed we finally had arrived at *just-in-time* (JIT) *learning.* Although we had definitely moved training closer to our performers than ever before, we soon realized that we hadn't achieved the true JIT promise we'd hoped. We made a classic mistake in that we confused the availability of learning with its ability to support learning in the moment of Apply. Although e-learning is a very powerful form of online training, most e-learning assets are not Performance Support.

The Importance of Context and Immediacy

There are two key characteristics that typically prevent e-learning from fulfilling this need—context and immediacy.

E-learning often follows a formal learning construct. The intent is to teach, which meets only the first two moments of need outlined in Chapter 2: when learning for the first time and when learning more. Each learning unit or topic begins with a broad objective and ends with specific steps and/or a practice. The performers are often assessed for mastery throughout the experiences. Their participation may be tracked or graded based on how much of the course they complete. The content is organized in a linear fashion with one lesson systematically following another, and often topics are introduced in a sequence that moves from simple to complex. These are sound learning design principles, but unfortunately they are also the reason this doesn't work well as a Performance Support learning asset.

The second characteristic that prevents e-learning from being an effective Performance Support tool is the way it is accessed and navigated. In order to track and manage e-learning, it is generally housed in what's called a *learning management system* (LMS). An LMS serves a vital role in allowing e-learning to be distributed, tracked, and reported in a very powerful way. Most LMSs are constructed in a library format. Once performers enter, they can search through lists of courses to find the correct curriculum needed for their learning needs. A particular curriculum can be required or recommended based on the performers' job roles or a number of other variables. Assessments can be administered, graded, and tracked. Many LMSs have grown to include other types of learning assets such as classroom schedules, videos, and even podcasts. The goal is to make formal instruction readily available for the performers at their desktops so they can access these training assets when needed. As was mentioned earlier, having access to a learning asset does not equate to Performance Support. Although the e-learning hosted on an LMS is available at any time, the journey to find each asset and navigate the LMS environment is not conducive to meeting a Performance Support need. With all this said, it doesn't mean that e-learning can't be a part of an overall PS strategy. It simply means that it does not stand alone as a PS strategy in and of itself.

Probably the two most important characteristics that differentiate Performance Support from any other learning discipline relate to context and immediacy. PS must be able to quickly support performers in the context of their doing their work. Immediacy is key, not just accessibility. The performers need to have the answer or support within seconds, not minutes or hours. They also need it within the context of their work.

The Performance Support solution needs to understand who the performers are and where they are having the problem, and it must be able to suggest answers in varying degrees of complexity depending on the performers' needs. The more embedded, intuitive, and tailored the support is, the higher the probability that the performers will see value in it and will engage it again at another time. This is why e-learning failed to meet the JIT promise outlined above. The performers often had to leave the work context to log in to their LMS and then engage in a fairly involved process to find the right learning asset. If the need was to learn, e-learning served the purpose. If the need was to support, e-learning often failed.

For PS to be successful, it needs to follow a defined framework. This framework can be either IT system based, nonsystem based, or both depending on the roles of the performers and the tasks being completed. In the system example, the framework should be embedded within the application itself as well as available as a standalone application on the desktop. This is called an *electronic Performance Support system* (EPSS). The reason for needing both is that there are times when a performer will require support when working in the system, and there will be times when they will need to be directed to the system based on a particular workflow or business process. PS assets that are embedded only within the application assume that the performers are at the right places and asking the right questions. This is not always the case. There are also times when performers need to access a system, or multiple systems, based on a particular workflow or business process.

Nonsystem support is also needed, such as remembering and following company policies, or how to walk through a particular talk-script. This type of content can also be hosted within a PS framework. Since these frameworks have no specific system in which to be embedded, they can exist as standalone applications on the desktop, be paper based, or they can be hosted on a mobile device, or they can exist as a combination of all three. The form factor a PS framework takes—that is, the format used for the PS framework—should be dictated by the way in which it will be consumed. Again, it gets back to context and immediacy. For example, if a salesperson is being supported by a PS framework, it may be best to provide that support in a paper-based job aid for review before entering a client meeting, on his laptop for immediate access when on the road, or even on his mobile device to be discussed when sitting with a customer. The key in each instance is that the information needed is available in the context of the problem and can be found immediately based on the need.

A truly integrated, impactful PS framework support can support both system and nonsystem instances at the same time. Many support needs require performers to navigate between both system and nonsystem tasks while completing a particular work objective. A PS framework would be needed both within each system and nonsystem stage as well as across the overarching workflow. A PS asset that was embedded only within each system would ignore the overall workflow and not support the critical nonsystems steps in between.

The Inverted Pyramid

Just as there are methods for guiding performers through formal instruction, the same can apply to the journey through Performance Support. As mentioned above, one of the shortcomings of many Performance Support assets is the way in which they are organized or designed. Many either offer the wrong amount of information, or they lead with the wrong type of learning asset, often confusing the performers or leaving them feeling overwhelmed. This was the downfall of many corporate learning portals in the 1990s. Although these Web sites attempted to be one-stop shops for many of the learning assets found within an organization, many were simply a sea of Web links to random learning assets, and they lacked the structure and context to make them effective.

Designing the appropriate journey through the many Performance Support assets needed to solve a problem can be equally as important as the information made available. When designing a PS solution or approach, we recommend using a design construct called the *inverted pyramid*. As is shown in Figure 5.1, the inverted pyramid is a direct complement to how performers are already being supported on the formal side.

When designing formal instruction and supporting the first two moments of need, the performers have little to no background in the content being taught. They need some type of overview with which to gain the appropriate perspective and context. For that purpose we typically start with learning objectives and demonstrations. These two areas help ground the performers in the conceptual underpinnings and reasons for engaging in the content about to be taught. Without this, there is little foundation upon which to build understanding and mastery. From there we journey into a deeper explanation and explore the details surrounding the specific area being taught. Finally we introduce them to the steps needed to complete the tasks. At this point there may be some type of review or practice to check for comprehension, and then the entire process is repeated. This process is represented by the triangle or pyramid shown at the top of Figure 5.1.

Although this is a very powerful model for formal instruction, the

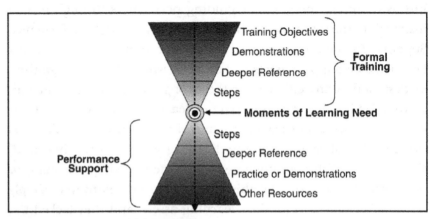

Figure 5.1. The Inverted PS Pyramid

same sequence breaks down when used for Performance Support. Because of the circumstances facing performers during an Apply moment, starting with broad objectives and working down through steps isn't contextual or timely enough. This is one of the reasons a classroom workbook that is such a wonderful formal learning asset often breaks down when used as a resource for Performance Support. Although the correct information is somewhere between the covers, the method of retrieving it and the sequence in which it is presented does not make it a practical Performance Support asset. Unfortunately, many wonderful textbooks and binders, although very helpful and essential when used in class, sit idle on shelves once performers return to the workplace. The form factor and design just don't meet the need any longer.

A Performance Support framework takes an inverted approach to the one just outlined. When performers are in an Apply moment, or in one of the last three moments of need, they need support as quickly and contextually as possible. When performers invoke a PS solution, the first things presented are the steps needed to help them perform a particular task as quickly as possible. These steps should be as specific and simplified as possible. Be careful of adding too much detail or overusing graphics at this point. The fewer distractions and extraneous information in the PS solution at this level, the better. The goal is to help the performers get back on track as quickly as possible. A common error made during this stage is to add too much extra text such as tips, elaborate definitions, or distracting graphics. We simply overwhelm the performers too soon in the support journey. This level should be written from the standpoint that, given very concise information, the answers will become apparent to the performers quickly.

The second layer is an extension of the first. Not all questions will be answered through steps. There are times when the performers need a deeper understanding. For the steps to make sense and become transferable, the performers may need the conceptual underpinning to a particular problem, the definition of certain terms, or a screenshot showing an example. This is where the deeper reference level comes in. Its role is to help clarify and extend the information offered in the steps layer.

If these first two levels are designed effectively, the majority of the performers' questions will be answered through them. There will still be times, however, when even richer or more robust resources are needed. This is where the final two layers come in. The next layer typically involves using demonstrations, simulations, and rich practices to help the performers internalize and understand the steps to support their learning. Notice that with each layer, the performers will need to commit a greater amount of both time and resources. They are also systematically moving further and further away from the task at hand and the immediate need they are trying to meet. That's why their having access to the entire framework is so important and why leading with the first two levels outlined above is also important. Too many Performance Support frameworks lead with these more robust and distancing assets. Doing this only moves the performers further from their immediate need and will discourage them from using the PS assets in the first place.

The fourth and final level, the resource level, is the gateway to other learning assets and related information. These assets should be linked as closely as possible to the specific step they are supporting, to minimize the performers' need to search or filter through too much information. For example, if there is a particular page on a Web site that supports a specific step, the framework should link directly to that page, not simply drop the performers at the home page expecting them to drill down from there. The same thing can be done with specific links to learning objects within e-learning courses, simulations (for example, Captivate demonstrations), links to related topics in a *community of practice* (CoP), and even supporting pdf documents or PowerPoint decks. Although the first three levels of the inverted pyramid are the most self-directed and efficient layers of the framework, there are also times when performers will need more anecdotal and in-depth support than these first three layers can provide. This is why the fourth level is so vital to the overall experience. It is the gatekeeper to these more elaborate, and often formal, learning assets.

The fourth level should be the line of last defense. It should be used only when the first three layers do not meet the need. Many learning and support cultures are not built around a self-service model, and in these settings, many performers will simply call a help desk or bother a peer before they attempt using the first three levels. This behavior can be redirected through an effective change management program that teaches the performers the benefits of navigating the framework first rather than jumping immediately to a peer or help desk. Part of this change management effort will be to encourage peers and help desks to redirect the performers back to the tools supporting the first three layers whenever possible. This will reinforce the effectiveness of the overall framework and help change the performers' behavior to one that defaults to the self-service levels first. Clearly this is a change that will take time and support at all levels of the organization, including senior management and the training department itself.

The Role of a PS Broker

Just as the e-learning world needed to adopt a system to host, track, and administer its content, the same is true for Performance Support. When supporting a performer across all five moments of need, it is rare to find a PS strategy that is defined by only one or two learning assets. When designing a PS solution, you will discover that you have many Performance Support assets that your performers will need access to depending on the complexity of the problem they are trying to solve or where they are in the work process. The LMS equivalent for PS is what's called a *PS broker*.

A PS broker's role is to make the right assets available in the right context and in the right sequence. In other words, a PS broker follows the inverted pyramid design outlined above. Like LMSs, a broker is an electronic tool that can either sit on performers' desktops or be embedded into a systems application. Even though PS brokers are electronic, they can support all types of learning content from IT applications such as SAP's to business skills such as sales training or leadership skills. They can also be hosted on multiple platforms such as desktop PCs, laptops, and even mobile devices. The device platform should be determined by the one that best fits into the context of the performers' workflow. It is possible to have a need for more than one output format. For instance, a sales representative may want to access a PS broker on her laptop when in her office or on her mobile phone if she is in the field. A PS broker should accommodate both environments whenever possible.

A PS broker hosts one of two types of content. The first is *internal content* that is often authored and maintained directly within the broker itself. Many of the broker tools that are available today are also authoring tools in and of themselves. This allows the designers and content owners to have a single repository of PS content that they can manage by themselves or with other stakeholders, such as subject-matter experts (SMEs), from directly within the lines of business, to help create and maintain the content.

One of the challenges of managing PS content is keeping it current. Many of the standard maintenance procedures used to update formal content won't work in the PS domain. The main reason for this is that the content is too dynamic and is often owned within the business units themselves. It would be unrealistic to ask learning departments or designers to keep up with all the potential changes. Brokers allow this maintenance work to be shared across all the individuals who need to be involved. The nice part about this approach is that the designers can set up the initial PS frameworks and let the SMEs simply maintain the content going forward. The SMEs do not need to have a design background. Depending on the complexity of the content or size of the change, some type of oversight may be needed on the part of the designers, but not nearly as rigorous as is needed on the formal side.

The second type of content supported by PS brokers is *external content*. Many organizations will discover that they already possess a number of very powerful learning assets that are either difficult to access or are poorly positioned relative to their level of effectiveness. This external content can be in many different forms. Some of the most common include these:

- Documents in pdf formats
- Documents in Microsoft Word, Excel, or PowerPoint formats
- Video files
- Audio files
- Simulations
- Reference-based Web sites
- Communities of practice (CoPs), blogs, and wikis
- E-learning modules
- Mentors, coaches, or help desk personnel

The power in linking out to these resources lies in the ease of maintaining these learning assets since the content continues to be updated by the content owners within the line of business.

Even though most brokers have authoring capabilities, there are times when it is not practical to embed the content. For example, working circumstances may make it impossible to have SMEs have access to or need to learn a new authoring environment. They may already be maintaining content elsewhere that is also used for other purposes. This content may already be housed in a content management system (CMS) or a knowledge base, or it may even be an e-learning lesson hosted in an LMS. Another example might be an existing vibrant CoP Web site that is hosting rich content and that has an environment for posting, editing, and maintaining content which is already familiar to all who contribute to it. For these, and many other reasons, a broker should link out to and host these already established and effective learning assets. The power of this hosting is not in creating the content but in making it accessible in the most effective and contextual way.

Here's an example of a broker in action. We recently worked with an organization that was in the process of rolling out a number of new products to their field sales representatives. In the past they would have brought the sales force in for several days of face-to-face classroom training where they would have been given a paper-based binder containing everything from the overall sales process to specific pricing and competitive information. There were also many Web resources and other marketing and sales documents supporting this rollout. The three main problems with this approach were that the representatives often left the training overwhelmed, they couldn't recall the information when asked to apply it in the context of their workflow, and they had a very difficult time keeping up with all the changes to the information that occurred in the weeks that followed class.

This was a perfect application for a broker. The organization constructed a PS broker that guided the performers through the appropriate support assets based on need and where they were in the sales process. The company still offered face-to-face training, but management was able to shorten it considerably and offer some of it virtually rather than bringing everyone into one location. The training experience was redesigned to include the PS broker as the main source of information during the training, and it was taught as a front-line support tool. Once they left the training, the sales represenatives had direct access to the resource links, and they were always provided the most up-to-date information. Due to the nature of the sales force's work lifestyle, the broker was provided on three platforms: a paper-based user guide, an EPSS version for their laptops, and a mobile version for their mobile phones. Each platform was published from the same source content and brokered the same links to the external content.

The key to this design was that the broker put the right amount of information in the hands of the sales representatives at the right time. It didn't overwhelm, and it let the performers control the flow and complexity of the information. This is the key characteristic of a successful PS broker. It doesn't just make information available. It guides the availability of Performance Support assets in a way that best fits the moment of Apply when encountered in the work context.

The Need for Multiple Paths

In order for a broker to provide the correct guidance, it needs to be engaged by the performers at the correct starting point or point of reference. As has been stated throughout this chapter, context is key. While PS content should always be fully searchable, filtering the content by predefined variables helps move the most appropriate learning assets closer to the moment of need they are attempting to serve. This is best achieved by designing the PS brokers so they are embedded into the work context. When applicable, this context needs to be viewed from up to four perspectives: workflow, job role, task, or unique identifiers. These context areas are interdependent in nature and design, and no single area is more important than another. One can browse or search by role and then by a unique identifier, or by workflow and then by job role.

Workflow Context

Workflow context in a PS framework allows the performers to access help based on a particular stage within a workflow. Process flows or workflow diagrams are some of the best tools to help in this area. For example, a sales representative may need to complete the sales process shown in Figure 5.2 in order to better sell to a customer.

Sales representatives may be familiar with individual steps within the process, but they may be struggling because they do not understand or know how to navigate through the overarching workflow. If the process is provided within the PS broker, the performers can better support themselves by identifying a task within a workflow, the steps that preceded it, and those that follow it. This will help them better comprehend how and why it is necessary to complete the current step and to facilitate the successful completion of the next steps.

Job Role Context

Job role context enables performers to filter content and other related PS assets based on their job roles and responsibilities. This navigational technique is most effective when an organization has

Figure 5.2. An Example of a Sales Process

well-defined and understood job roles or functions within it. Figure 5.3 shows sample roles that exist within a call center.

As identified in this graphic, a person in any of these roles could quickly identify his role, which then would either display the processes in which he was involved or list the tasks he needs to complete. Roles or functions could also be embedded in organizations, departments, or other "who am I" identifiers that would facilitate effective and efficient access to the required information.

Task Context

Task contexts are typically formed as categorical lists of procedures. These can be further categorized by subtask, roles, workflow, or other unique identifiers. The intent is that if performers need to search or browse, they can easily access a list of procedures that they may be required to complete. Although this is not the typical preferred method to access PS objects (due to lack of role or process orientation), it is usually easy to provide this navigational scheme with the objects cross-referenced under other containers. You may also use this technique when documenting the features and functions of a system without regard to the environment in which it will be used.

When considering a PS strategy, the use of task context is often misunderstood in relationship to the overall framework, and it is frequently given too much emphasis. This is easy to understand since the tasks are ultimately the "answers" performers may be looking for. With that said, tasks should not stand alone without considering the other structure types listed here. If the PS strategy is based on only a task context support structure, the tasks themselves can become overwhelming, misunderstood, and difficult to find. It is key to balance this type of context support with at least one of the other three to offer a complete PS experience.

Unique Identifier Context

The unique identifier contexts are based on the specific nature of your organization, and they should be immediately recognizable by

Service Desk Agent	Incident Manager	Incident Handler	Problem Handler	Change Coordinator	Change Handler

Figure 5.3. An Example of Job Roles at a Call Center

the target audience. For example, an organization may categorize information by products it sells, services it renders, or systems it uses across a number of workflows. The goal is to provide unique identifiers in addition to the other typical identifiers (roles, workflows, and tasks) as another option to assist in the efficient navigation of the PS offering.

It is imperative that PS designers understand what, if any, unique identifiers exist and how the users will identify with them at the point of need. For example, some unique identifiers we have seen used in the past are product types, services offered, or sales programs that would be found within or across certain roles in the organization. The structure shown in Figure 5.4 is one that pivots on consumer products within a retail hardware store. These unique identifiers that span multiple roles, workflows, and tasks would be found in the layer beneath.

Integrating the Four Context Perspectives

To effectively design for the different perspectives, you need to modify your current task analysis and resulting design tasks. Most task analysis processes focus on only those tasks that need to be completed and the sequence in which it makes sense to teach them. This is based on categorical grouping of like tasks, prerequisite knowledge, building in complexity, and to some degree, the preferences of the designers.

Livestock Production	Feed and Companion Animals	Country Lifestyles	Buildings and Building Supplies	Tools and Shop Supplies	Petroleum Supplies	Grain Production

Figure 5.4. An Example of Unique Task Identifiers Related to Consumer Products within a Retail Hardware Store

In addition, your PS broker will need to initially consider all four of the content structures outlined above each time a new learning initiative is started. The reasoning for this is that users will not always access PS in a sequential manner, nor will they have the prerequisite knowledge to perform. Another way to look at it is that PS should be created not on how performers would learn something but on how they identify their work context at the moment of need. This leads to a greater need for modular design that is accessible based on the users' needs and orientations.

For example, when claims agents answer the phone, their orientation is not task based. Instead, they are thinking in terms of how their current place in the claims entry process relates to the type of call they are answering. These agents would want to find the appropriate task context information based on an overarching process flow. This may involve system and nonsystem tasks depending on where the associate is in the process. Without this layer, the scope of possible tasks is too great. The process layer helps filter the task content that follows. The steps to ensure that you've included one or more of these four context perspectives into your analysis and design process are as follows:

1. **Focus on the business processes.** During your task analysis, rather than just obtaining a list of tasks and prioritizing them, have the SME walk you through the business process that needs to be supported. As you move through the process, ask questions pertaining to what tasks support it, how they are done, and where it may be natural for people to look for support.
2. **Understand the job roles related to tasks and business processes.** Instead of just listing job roles and the tasks they contain, relate them back to the business processes. Also understand how performers would identify themselves at the point of need. Is it by role, function, or some other "who am I" identifier?
3. **Ask about unique identifiers.** Identify questions that

end users will ask at the point of need, and find out what unique identifiers they identify with beyond tasks, roles, or processes. Determine whether these identifiers are subsets of another perspective or if they should stand on their own. If the latter, determine what navigational scheme best supports the items and how they may be shared or linked with others.

Guidelines for Broker Interface Design

Here are five guidelines to consider then designing a PS broker.

1. Determine the Work Context of Your Performer

The first thing to determine is the work environment in which your audience will be interfacing with the broker. The more embedded the broker can be within the workflow, the better. You will need to understand the technology available to your performers in the context of completing their work. Do you have a mobile audience who relies on mobile phones and laptops or one that works primarily at stationary workstations or desktops? Does the broker support an IT application, business skills, or both?

Even though the main focus may to be system based, many still involve an overarching business process that may have nonsystem tasks such as meeting with a manager, dealing with customers, or submitting forms to HR. These nonsystem tasks need to be represented in the broker as well. If the broker is supporting an IT application, you will need to determine to what degree you can embed the broker directly into the application. This will often involve working with your IT department or the vendor who created the application. The closer you can embed the broker into specific screens or menus, the higher the probability that the performers will actually use the tool. If you are not able to embed the broker, then a desktop-only tool can still be developed.

2. Determine Whether to Host Existing Content or to Author New Assets

A broker can either aggregate existing content, or it can allow you to author, and then host, your own. You will need to perform a learning asset analysis (see below) to determine which existing content you will be able to leverage through the broker and which content you'll need to build from scratch. Be careful not to assume that all existing assets are appropriate in their current form or that they are designed well. Be sure you examine each asset to see that it supports the process, tasks, and steps you discovered in your rapid task analysis. There may be times when you'll need to divide a learning asset into smaller chunks that can be better accessed based on the complexity of the process or the performers' specific needs. When brokering assets such as e-learning modules, you will want to link as deeply into the individual learning object layers as you can.

3. Determine the Appropriate Support Level for Each PS Learning Asset and Content Type

As was explained earlier, the power of a broker is its ability to make PS learning assets available at increasingly higher levels within the inverted pyramid based on its depth of content and complexity. After you've completed your rapid task analysis and learning asset analysis, you need to determine which content area and external learning asset will be accessed at which level. The step level tends to be one that requires the most amount of authoring whereas the resources level typically hosts external content such as Web sites, pdf documents, and e-learning modules.

4. Determine a Maintenance and Feedback Strategy

A broker is only as effective as the content contained within it. One of the most common challenges faced when maintaining a broker over time is keeping the content current. Due to the contextual nature of this content and the fact that many of the learning assets are aggregated from other areas within the organization, it is critical to identify and manage all the content owners involved.

Whether the content is being pulled from external sources or is being maintained directly within the broker's authoring system, both a maintenance strategy and a schedule will need to be employed that are realistic and sustainable for all involved. You will also want to create a way for the performers to provide feedback on the content. This feature can be built into the broker itself through strategies such as a rating or e-mail system. The PS broker will also need to be maintained as a standalone system and architecture. Typically this is determined by the performers' technical setups. Will the PS broker be accessed through the Internet or an internal network? Is it standalone, freestanding, or both? If the performers are not on a network, or if they are disconnected at different times, you will need to initiate a replication strategy that will update the broker at times when the performers have access to the network or at other times and through some other types of versioning processes.

5. Determine the Appropriate Use of Graphics

The graphical nature of the PS broker can help with navigation and recall. Graphics need to be employed in the most effective and least distracting way. There are a few guiding principles to consider:

1. If graphics are used during formal training, they should be reused in the PS broker for recall.
2. Limit the use of graphics for the sake of "decoration." Attempt to make them as meaningful and engaging as possible.
3. Balance the use of graphics throughout the PS broker based on need and impact. There typically are few graphics found at the step level of the inverted pyramid. The use of graphics tends to increase as the performers dig deeper into the other layers and their use becomes more powerful.
4. Screenshots are typically introduced at the deeper reference level of a broker.

5. Process and workflow diagrams are critical graphics for navigation throughout a broker.

6. Follow standard *user interface* (UI) *principles* when designing navigation. Apply these principles in the placement, consistency, and layout of icons and navigation buttons. Developing consistent "look and feel" sets can help with this issue.

HOW TO MAKE IT WORK FOR YOU

Most organizations have a plethora of learning assets embedded in the full spectrum of possible modalities. This is because our profession has a insatiable appetite for pursuing new and better ways of enabling learning within the organization.

As mentioned in this book's preface, this pursuit has been lopsided in its attention to the formal side of learning. But now as you go about setting your sights on the moment of Apply, this becomes an excellent time to take inventory of all your learning assets and determine how well they play across the full spectrum of learning requirements in the organization.

Conduct a Learning Asset Inventory

This is a good time to determine the degree to which the existing assets meet the learning requirements at all five moments of need. The process for doing this is called the *learning asset inventory*. Here's how you go about it.

Task 1. Identify All the Types of Learning Assets You Currently Offer throughout the Organization

A learning type is defined by the nature of content and/or how the learning asset is housed and delivered to the performers. Table 5.1 lists the learning asset types identified during a learning asset inven-

Table 5.1. An Example of an Inventory of Current Learning Assets

Learning Asset	Key
1. Case studies	CS
2. Coaching	CO
3. E-reference	ER
4 E-role play	RP
5. FAQs	FA
6. Help desk	HD
7. Instructor-led training (ILT) (classroom)	ILT
8. Knowledge channel	KC
9. Job aid	JA
10. Learning portal	LP
11. Policy and procedure (P&P) guides	PP
12. Podcasts	P
13. Recorded webinars	RW
14. Reference materials	RM
15 SIMs	SI
16. Structured on-the-job training (OJT)	SO
17. Visual and audio ILT	VA
18. Virtual class (VILT)	VC
19. Web-based training (WBT)	WBT
20. Wikis	WI

tory. For every type, the organization has instances of those assets with learning content embedded within them. This is the first task in the learning asset analysis process.

Task 2. Rate the Contribution Value of Each Asset Type

This contribution value is determined by determining the current and possible contribution value of each asset at each of the five moments of need.

Table 5.2. An Example of the Contribution Value Ratings for Several Types of Learning Assets

Asset Type	1 Learn New		2 Learn More		3 Apply		4 Solve		5 Change	
C = Current **P = Potential**	C	P	C	P	C	P	C	P	C	P
Coaching	2	5	2	6	4	7	0	7	0	5
Role play	5	7	5	7	0	0	0	3	0	5
Instructor-led training (ILT) (classroom)	7	7	7	7	0	0	0	0	0	3
Virtual classroom (VILT)	2	7	2	7	0	0	0	2	0	7
Job aids	2	7	2	7	3	7	0	7	2	7
Structured on-the-job training (OJT)	3	5	3	5	3	5	1	5	1	5
Web-based training (WBT)	5	6	5	6	0	6	0	4	0	6

Table 5.2 shows what this rating might look like for several of the asset types.

Task 3. Consolidate or Remove Where Possible

In every case when we have helped organizations with their asset analysis, we have identified assets that are playing redundant roles. In most of these cases, we have consolidated them into a single asset type fulfilling that role. Sometimes the redundant roles still contribute because of unique requirements within the organization. But in principle the number of duplicate assets should be merged into a stronger single asset type.

For example, in Table 5.2, the structured on-the-job training plays a redundant role with coaching, job aids, and Web-based training. It could readily be dropped from the offering.

Task 4. Strengthen Asset Potential and Add What Is Missing

As you can see in the learning asset ratings in Table 5.2, most of the assets are failing to deliver the full potential they offer. A final step in this asset analysis is to evaluate the instructional integrity of these various assets and, according to their potential contribution to learning, put in place a plan for strengthening them. See http://performersupport.ning.com for an example of a tool we have developed to assess the instructional integrity of an asynchronous self-learning system.

* * *

Learning asset analysis helps you know what you have, what you should remove from the current offering, what needs to be strengthened instructionally, and what's missing. If your organization is typical, you have redundant asset types in the first two moments of need, and you do not have the appropriate asset types in the final three moments of need (Apply, Solve, Change.) As you work to apply the principles presented in this chapter and move through the rest of this book with the same intent, you will find insights to help you know how to add what is missing and redesign and thereby strengthen what you have.

Conduct an Access Analysis

Fundamental to the success of any PS broker are the ways in which it provides access to the learning asset and related information hosted within. As has been discussed throughout this chapter, a broker's primary responsibility is to make the most helpful and appropriate support available as quickly as possible. The journey through the inverted pyramid is more than simply offering random support from the step level down. Rather, it needs to be designed in such a way that allows it to lead with the appropriate steps in the first place. Conducting an *access analysis* can help you decide on the correct design components needed to create these critical access points.

Imagine that you had gathered 10,000 electronic copies of the best recipes from award-winning chefs throughout the world. Your next job is to make those recipes easily available to anyone attempting to prepare them. What categories might you consider when doing that? Here are a few groupings that might work:

- Recipes that serve three or fewer people
- Recipes based on particular ingredients
- Recipes grouped by dietary needs
- Recipes grouped by the amount of time it takes to prepare them
- Recipes that are best served during certain holiday seasons
- Recipes based on the expertise of the chef attempting to prepare them, from beginner to expert
- Recipes that are considered to be part of a particular type of cuisine

In this example, there could be hundreds of categories that could be used to present these recipes. Selecting the best ones depends on the needs of the chefs you are attempting to support.

The same is true when creating access points to a PS broker. Although there may be countless ways to grant access to the learning assets you have gathered, there are only certain ones that are more helpful than others based on the performer population you have been tasked with supporting. Following the steps outlined below will help you conduct an effective access analysis that will enable you to discover and design these access points.

Task 1. Gather the Correct Stakeholders

The stakeholders needed when performing an access analysis need to be representative of the business environment and daily workflow in which the PS broker will be accessed. We often call these individuals *business-matter experts* (BMEs). Although SMEs may have been helpful in other stages of the design process, they are often not the best candidates for this particular type of analysis.

For example, an SME may have expertise with a particular IT system being designed, but she may have little understanding of the business environment and related problems encountered when using this application in the context of the workflow. BMEs, on the other hand, are the true end users, and although they may have little expertise in the system, they understand the work context in which problems arise and the business outcomes that need to be met. At times a BME and an SME may be one and the same individual. If that is the case, it is critical that this individual understand the role he or she is being asked to play when assisting with this type of analysis. SMEs will often be led by feature and function and not by outcome and application, and outcome and application is the driving factor during this stage in the development process.

Task 2. Define the Appropriate Access Categories

Ask as many of the following questions as needed based on the type of PS broker being designed and the BMEs being represented:

1. Is there a particular overarching business process that is followed when completing a particular business outcome? Are there business processes nested within this overarching business process?
2. What are the different roles involved in completing a particular outcome or business process? What is their relationship to one another?
3. Are there any specific business problems that are typically encountered when working through a particular outcome? Are these issues unique to the roles defined above?
4. What are the most common help desk or support call questions asked to support a particular business outcome?
5. Are there certain products or services that need to be supported? If so, is there a priority of importance, frequency of need or use, or degree of difficulty associated with any of these?
6. Are there different types of customers that need to be supported? If so, are there any unique needs or business issues related to these customer types?

Task 3. Prioritize These Access Categories Based on Their Effectiveness

Once these categories are identified, they should be prioritized based on the performers' needs being served. When the broker is being accessed, it is key that performers are greeted with the most helpful and common categories that help them address their moment of need. Workflow processes and job roles are the most common categories we have seen in the PS brokers we have developed.

Task 4. Use the Identified Access Points to Guide Performers Most Effectively

Architect the PS broker to best introduce and guide with these access points. Just as a classroom workbook is structured around a table of contents, such is the case with the use of these key access points and your PS broker.

These leading categories become the outline and architecture for your PS brokers and the performers' journey through it. Although there should always be a search capability in every broker, if designed correctly, the categories discovered during an access analysis activity will become the guide in supporting your performers. It is common to have more than one category in a single PS broker. For example, you may use a workflow diagram as the landing page because it was the most common guide to answering your performers' questions, but you may also include a page or link to learning assets grouped by a list of products. This will be determined by the prioritization listed above.

INSIGHTS FROM A THOUGHT LEADER: Dr. Maggie Martinez

Dr. Margaret (Maggie) Martinez, CEO of the Training Place (www.trainingplace.com), has worked in the fields of learning, information, and technology for more than 20 years. Previously she was the worldwide training and certification director for the WordPerfect Corporation. Martinez is a respected consultant on adult learning methodologies and strategies, and she is considered an expert in the area of learning orientation and intentional learning research—that is, the study of how people learn differently and most effectively.

Martinez plays an active role in helping organizations assess performer proficiency and design and deliver highly personalized learning solutions. She has provided leadership, insight, and perspective on adaptive learning issues important to the federal government and major corporations worldwide as they cope with diverse challenges—including rapidly changing business opportunities, the need to move performers' learning via Internet-based technology, the need to promote continual learning and performance improvement, and the pace of accelerated technological advancement.

Dr. Martinez's academic initiatives have focused on demystifying the world of learning and performance by pioneering individual learning differences and personalization research integrated with recent advances in the neurosciences. She uses the research to build blended learning frameworks and solutions that recognize, match, and support critical factors that influence how individuals can learn more successfully. This research explores the powerful impact of emotions and intentions on learning and performance, and it uses tools to assess online learning ability.

Martinez has a doctorate in instructional psychology and technology, and she regularly presents at major conferences. She also publishes in academic and trade publications. She is a board member for the Alpine Testing Solutions company, and she is on the advisory board for the Greater Arizona eLearning Association.

The Learning Orientation Research

The *Learning Orientation (LO) Research* discusses the theoretical and neuroscience foundations for understanding sources of individual differences in learning. It specifically explores the important impact of emotions, intentions, and social factors on learning. Discoveries in the neurosciences in the last 10 years have revealed the extraordinary complexities of brain activity and the multiple aspects of the influences on the thinking processes. These theories highlight and explore the importance of understanding the influence of emotions and intentions on learning, performance, memory, and decision making.

The *LO Research* explores how three primary factors impact intentional learning success and influence the development of individual learning differences:

1. The *learning independence domain (autonomy) factor* considers the locus of control and refers to individuals' desires and abilities to take responsibility, to make choices, to control, manage, and improve their own learning, and to self-assess (that is, make choices independent of the instructor or prescribed sequences) in the attainment of goals.

2. The *committed strategic planning and learning effort domain factor* refers to the degree to

which performers plan, persist, and commit deliberate, strategic purpose and effort to accomplish learning and to achieve goals.

3. The *self-motivation factor (the desire or will to learn or achieve mastery)* refers to individuals' intrinsic passion, desire, and/or striving to learn. It considers the performers' general will, commitment, intent, drive, or passion for improving, mastering, transforming, and setting and achieving goals, taking risks, and meeting challenges.

Learning Orientations (Dispositions to Learn)

The learning orientation model uses the three-factor construct to explore four specific learning orientations or dispositions to learn. *Learning orientations* refers to the ways in which individuals, with varying beliefs and levels of abilities, will intentionally and emotionally approach, commit, and expend effort to some extent, and then experience learning to progress and attain goals. Learning orientations describe individuals' proclivity to take control, expend strategic effort, manage resources, and take risks to learn. In other words, learning orientations describe how individuals typically want and choose to use and manage their brain. The learning orientations help us understand how and why individuals learn and perform differently.

There are four primary learning orientations:

- Transforming
- Performing
- Conforming
- Resistant

The following is an explanation of each of these dispositions.

Transforming Performers

Transforming performers place great importance on personal strengths, abilities, persistent efforts, strategies, high standards, learning efficacies, self-assessments, and positive expectations. As they acquire expertise, transforming performers enjoy sharing knowledge or coaching or mentoring others.

Transforming learning is a skilled, adaptive approach that encourages and supports positive anticipations, expertise building, risk taking, exploratory experiences, holistic thinking, mentoring relationships, self-directed problem solving, performer-controlled opportunities, high learning standards, and achievement of challenging personal goals for long-term accomplishments and change. For self-motivation with respect to learning, transforming performers seldom rely solely on short-term goals, deadlines, comparisons against other people's performance, or expected social or instructional compliance.

Performing Performers

In comparison, performing performers are less apt to take risks. They are skilled performers who consciously, systematically, and capably uses conative, affective, social, and cognitive processes, strategies, preferences, and self-regulated learning skills, such as note taking, rehearsal, mnemonics, memorization, and feedback-control processing, to achieve expected learning objectives and tasks.

In contrast to transforming performers, performing performers are more short term and task oriented, take fewer risks with challenging or difficult goals, focus on grades and normative achievement standards, and most often rely on coaching relationships and available external resources and influences to accomplish tasks or goals. Often, performing performers will clearly acknowledge meeting only the stated objectives, getting the grade, and avoiding exploratory steps beyond the requirements of the learning task.

For self-motivation with respect to learning, in contrast to conforming performers, performing performers seldom rely solely on compliance, comparisons with others, or explicit direction and feedback. Performing performers use more sophisticated learning skills and strategies and take some control and responsibility for their learning. Performing performers do not like to change rules, procedures, or systems that they are comfortable with and that they think already work well.

Conforming Performers

Compared to transforming or performing performers, conforming performers are more compliant, and they more passively accept knowledge, store it, and reproduce it to conform, complete assigned tasks if they can, and please others. The conforming performer does not typically think critically or analytically, synthesize feedback, or give knowledge new meaning to initiate change in themselves or the environment. These performers are typically less-skilled performers, and they have little desire to control or manage their learning or initiate change in their jobs or environment. Conforming performers believe that learning is necessary only when it helps them meet the requirements in their life. They prefer to expend minimum effort on simple goals that others set for them. Conforming performers are not comfortable with change, risk taking, or exploratory opportunities.

Resistant Performers

In contrast to the other three learning orientations, resistant performers lack a fundamental belief that learning and achievement can help them achieve personal goals or initiate positive change. Too often they have suffered repeated, long-term frustration from inappropriate learning situations. A series of unskilled, imperceptive instructors and unfortunate learning experiences has deterred resistant performers from enjoying learning experiences. Resistant performers do not believe in or use formal education or academic institutions as positive or enjoyable influences in their life.

Information about learning orientations can be found at:
www.trainingplace.com/source/research/learningorientations.htm

More information about the research can be found at:
www.trainingplace.com/source/research/index.html

FAQs can be found at:
www.trainingplace.com/loq/faq.htm

Learning Orientations and Performance Support Solutions

Good solutions that support organizational and learning excellence should also consider a variety of ways for a performer to "bridge" between the conventional, formal learning experiences and Performance Support efficiently. Good analysis should show how much or little Performance Support requirements are dependent upon different dispositions to learn or how solutions should focus on differences in individual, team, or work group performance. Good analysis should also consider a wide range of learning resources, such as Performance Support tools and brokers, to support individualized learning and performance.

When designing a PS solution, you need to consider not only which PS assets are needed based on the problem or work process but also how each performer may or may not use the asset differently—some more successfully than others. Such an approach considers what the outcomes of individual performers' experiences are supposed to be and which strategies help performers achieve their performance and learning goals—more effectively and efficiently.

In order for a PS broker to provide the correct guidance, it needs to engage the performers' attention and help them commit and persist toward success. During analysis, the broker role should consider different learning dispositions and help performers have efficient and effective access to multiple resources. The broker should understand that successful performers place great importance on the acts of striving, working with a purpose, and making a commitment to applying focused, strategic planning, hard-working effort, and high principles to learn. Less successful performers generally lack the insight that strategic planning and committed effort are contributing factors for achievement.

6

EMPLOYING THE STRENGTH
OF SOCIAL LEARNING

Knowledge is not simply another commodity. On the contrary. Knowledge is never used up. It increases by diffusion and grows by dispersion.

—Daniel J. Boorstin

A STORY TO GET STARTED:
THE POWER OF COMMUNITY, FROM BOB

When my mother turned 80 years old, my sisters and I decided to throw her a special family birthday party. As we started sharing different ideas for a gift, we arrived at the notion of a "memory box." We wanted to surprise her with a keepsake that would help her reconnect with friends and family she has known throughout her life. We decided to try and contact as many people as we could and ask them to record a short audio message on an online Web site. The messages would then be downloaded and played through a device resembling a music box. We wanted her to be able to listen to the stories of all the lives she had touched and friends she had made.

As you can imagine, once we began this quest, we quickly realized that most of the people we knew, or could remember, had moved away. Quite frankly, we weren't even sure how many were still alive!

So we determined we'd need to keep it small, and we ended up using an e-mail list of around 10 of her friends whom we knew she was staying in contact with.

That's where the power of community kicked in. Once this small group realized what we were trying to do, unbeknownst to us, they took it upon themselves to begin forwarding the e-mail to other friends of my mother that they had in their network. E-mails became blog postings, and blog postings found their way to other social networking sites. My sister called us a week later nearly in tears. When she checked the Web site, we had over a 100 recordings from people throughout the country who had known my mother from as far back as grade school.

I will never forget the look on her face as she listened to each voice. Each replayed a special event and memory in my mother's life just as if it were yesterday. Some sang songs, and others retold stories that had us laughing until we cried. The power of the social network we live in today came through in ways we could never have imagined.

Tapping into the collaborative power of this learning asset holds a potential beyond what most of us can yet imagine. What impact will it have on corporate learning structures, and how can it be maximized to meet all Five Moments of Learning Need?

This chapter explores the current options available and lays the groundwork for beginning this journey.

WHAT YOU NEED TO KNOW

Social learning has actually been around for as long as we have gathered in the workplace attempting to get things accomplished. It is only recently that this learning asset has gained in momentum due to the advent of the many technologies now available to host these conversations. These technologies have helped expand social learning beyond the days of shouting over a cubicle and gathering in the lunchroom to share ideas or seek an answer to a problem. These conversations can now span across cities, states, countries, and continents. Social learning takes collaboration to a whole new level by removing the two most significant barriers that have kept it from becoming as successful and powerful as it could be: time and space.

The one danger of becoming overly enamored with the technology side of this modality is that we can often miss out on, or begin ignoring, the full spectrum of all that makes up social learning. Just because we can currently collaborate with each other via technologies such as mobile phones and the Internet, we shouldn't underestimate the potential of a robust and vibrant collaborative community.

Categories of Social Learning

There are two categories of social learning: synchronous and asynchronous. These categories are not technology dependent; rather, they are experiential in nature. The *synchronous social learning approach* is one in which participants collaborate in real time. The *asynchronous social learning approach* is just the opposite. These exchanges are delayed, although the response time can be fairly immediate depending on the technology being used and the availability of the others participating. Social dialogues can be hosted in groups or one-on-one. Both synchronous and asynchronous collaborations can be captured, recorded, or archived depending on the platform being used. This allows for the reuse of content within a Performance Support framework or broker.

Synchronous Social Learning

The following are some of the most common approaches found within the synchronous social learning category.

Coaching or Mentoring Programs

A coaching or mentoring program typically consists of one or more individuals being assigned to a performer with the intent of guiding them through some type of learning experience. These interactions can include programs such as onboarding and leadership training. They can be highly structured or more informal in nature.

Online Chats

Online chat is a virtual technology that utilizes a Web-enabled host which allows two or more performers to carry on a conversation in real time. These applications are either free through services such as AOL Instant Messenger, Yahoo! Messenger, and Microsoft Messenger, or they can be included as part of commercial desktop applications and e-mail clients such as Lotus Notes and Microsoft Outlook. Beyond one-to-one or group text-based chats, many allow for the use of video, file transfers, and application sharing to enhance the experience. These chats can also be hosted on multiple platforms such as desktop PCs and mobile phones.

Virtual Training-Coaching Platforms

These technologies go beyond the chat experience and allow for a more robust learning exchange. As is the case with online chats, there are many free and commercial options. The most commonly used applications are Webex by Cisco, Adobe's Connect Pro, and Microsoft's LiveMeeting, just to name a few. These technologies are better positioned for hosting event types of experiences. Features such as sharing and annotating slides, group breakout rooms for private discussions, polling, and the chat capabilities mentioned above are all available depending on the tool being used. Although mobile clients are beginning to become more prevalent in this area, most virtual meetings are still hosted on some form of desktop or laptop PC.

Virtual Worlds

Virtual worlds take both online chat and virtual live meetings to a whole new level. Virtual worlds allow learners to meet as virtual characters, or avatars, in a simulated world enabling a host of collaborative learning experiences. These are highly powerful and immersive environments where performers can experience everything from simulating a state of emergency as a member of an emergency response team to attending a global sales conference with other sales representatives from around the world. They can walk, or even fly, through simulated landscapes and scenarios interacting with other avatars along the way—all without leaving their home or company office.

Asynchronous Social Learning

The following are some of the most common approaches found within the asynchronous social learning category.

Blogs

Blogs are Web sites that allow individuals to post their ideas, which can then be commented on by others. They are often thought of as a type of "virtual diary" that others are allowed to read and add feedback to. A blog can apply varying degrees of security, which can control who's allowed to view or comment on the posts. A blog's key differentiator is that the information is initiated and "owned" by an individual who then allows a community to react to it. Like all other technologies listed here, there are blogs that are available on free services and others that can be purchased, thus offering people and organizations varying degrees of customization and control.

Microblogs

Microblogging is a smaller and more immediate form of blogging. Microblogs limit the number of characters allowed in each exchange, forcing the interactions to become more conversational in nature. Although an individual may have a microblog Web site, a majority of the interactions occur through microblog clients that allow the responses to be tracked more quickly and in an organized manner. These clients can be PC based or hosted on a mobile device. Microblog postings can be replied to, reposted, and grouped by theme. Microblogs allow for the interactions to be much more highly focused and dynamic than do typical blogs. Like most social learning tools, any number of security settings can be invoked to control access and the level of engagement.

Wikis

A wiki is a Web site that allows a group of performers to collaborate on a shared set of ideas or topics. Unlike the blog mentioned above, the content found in a wiki is owned by all of its members. There is a shared responsibility to keep the information current and dynamic. As is true for blogs, there can be varying degrees of security used to control the flow of information. There is typically some type of monitoring occurring that helps keep the content credible and the engagement appropriate.

Social Networking Platforms

Social networking platforms are Web sites that combine any number of the tools listed above, both synchronous and asynchronous. They are typically initiated based on some type of theme or group dynamic. The number of tools used is based on the function of the group and the level of collaborations required. These Web sites can also host other resources such as podcasts, videos, pictures, and a number of other related information sources that would add value to the overall conversations being hosted. Although this last type seems the most robust and desirable, social learning is a world of balance, and overkill can actually inhibit collaboration if the interactions are not managed correctly.

Social Learning and Performance Support

As a learning industry, we tend to become enamored with trends and new learning "toys." In the 20 plus years that we have been involved in this industry, we have seen many new learning approaches that have held tremendous potential drift to the wayside and become obsolete or difficult to implement. Although some were simply not effective learning tools or strategies in the first place, many didn't survive because they weren't correctly incorporated into an already established learning culture and strategy. Unfortunately, we tend to be easily distracted by the shiny pennies. We spend years walking a particular path, developing an effective and integrated learning strategy that involves multiple learning assets blended across the five moments of need. All of a sudden a new trend comes along, and we take an immediate right turn, putting a significant amount of our resources and budget into this area while ignoring its implications on the work done to date. We also tend to implement first and ask questions later. Social learning has the potential of becoming the latest casualty if we fail to put it into the proper context relative to Performance Support as the overall discipline.

As was discussed in Chapter 5, Performance Support is an overarching approach to supporting performers across the five moments of need. It is not linked to any one asset or approach, but rather, it brokers the appropriate type of learning asset in the right context to meet the current learning need. Social learning, especially with the emerging technologies of today, has tremendous potential to play a vital role in an organization's overall Performance Support strategy if, like all other learning assets, it is positioned in the correct manner. Immediacy and context are the cornerstones of Performance Support. The danger of positioning social learning as the predominant asset for supporting your performers is that many of the current social learning categories outlined above do not possess these characteristics. Once again we run the risk of missing the potential of a powerful learning asset by poorly positioning it relative to the others we already have available.

If you consider the inverted pyramid design for PS brokers and frameworks, social learning fits best in the fourth and final layer of support (Figure 6.1). It is considered to be a more dependent and complex set of resources, and it can be accessed once the more direct and self-guided assets have been used. Remember, the optimal PS framework is one that starts by using more self-directed and efficient resources than those that are more involved and complex.

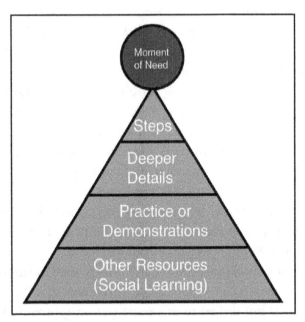

Figure 6.1. The Position of Social Learning in the PS Inverted Pyramid

The intent is to get the performer back to work as quickly as possible. Although social learning tools contain rich and powerful content, they are not the most efficient and self-directed resources available.

There are a number of ways social learning can be embedded into a broker framework. For example, if performers are being supported on a particular step in a sales process and the first three levels of support have not met their needs, the sales representatives are now ready to move beyond the primarily self-directed levels of support. They may be ready to access some type of social learning community that grants them access to their peers and other experts. A number of scenarios could be introduced at this point. First, a link to a chat environment could be offered directing the sales representatives to peers with specific expertise in this area. A second option could be that the performers be linked to specific page on a wiki where best practices and anecdotal recommendations are being shared surrounding this step in the sales process. Another option could involve simply supplying phone numbers or e-mail addresses of other peers who could help. The e-mail option could even go as far as launching the performers' e-mail client and prepopulating the "To" field with the experts' e-mail addresses and the subject line asking for help in this particular area. Finally, the performers could be directed to blogs authored by other sales representatives within the company who have expertise in this specific area. These are but a few of the ways social learning could be optimized in this situation.

Two key characteristics that make this type of embedding work are the level to which the linking occurs and the type of asset provided to support the problem at hand. In the scenario in which linking is being used, it's critical that the link go as deeply into the social learning tool as is possible. Simply dropping the performers off on the landing page of a wiki is not as effective as taking them within the wiki itself and linking them directly to a discussion on the topic being supported. If the performers are not taken this deeply into the social learning tool, they are less likely to do the searching and filtering themselves. The goal is to make the journey throughout these brokered assets as seamless and contextual as possible.

Not all social learning environments are created equal. Many differ in their ease of navigation, time to process, level of credibility, and availability of resources. If a performer needs a direct and reliable answer, a chat may provide greater access and a higher degree of interaction than a wiki, which would take a great amount of time to process and to receive a response from. On the other hand, if the type of support required needs to provide greater depth of content based on a larger community of input, then a wiki or blog may be best to solve the problem being addressed. The format needs to match the complexity of the problem and the time the performers have to solve it. Some social learning environments are more immediate and robust than others. This is where using the power of a broker to help guide the performers through these various options truly shines. These types of design decisions can be considered and offered through a brokered approach as opposed to simply making any and all social learning tools available and leaving it up to the performers to navigate correctly on their own. If left to their own, many choose poorly and become frustrated with the journey before they truly discover the power that these tools possess.

Guidelines for Building Social Learning Environments That Thrive

Social learning is not an "if you build it, people will come" environment. Many learning organizations are surprised at the amount of effort needed to create, launch, maintain, and sustain these communities. Although the premise sounds ideal, and although social networking environments have found huge success outside of the workplace, many have struggled to find a model that succeeds within the corporate work setting. Here are a few recommendations to help get social learning up and running as well as helping it thrive for as long as possible.

Use Project-Based Communities

Use project-based communities to help get things started. Some of the early efforts in social learning tried to entice performers to participate by grouping them by common job roles. The belief was that if we have performers who share a common background, the next natural step was that they would start sharing ideas and best practices within these disciplines. But many of these communities struggled to get off the ground and find any type of sustainable momentum. The fundamental problem was that the performers didn't see them as a valuable use of their time. If they are going to join these communities, they need to see a direct tie to their work output and productivity. Originally, it wasn't that they didn't see the potential of virtually joining their colleagues in these types of discussion. For many it was simply an issue of time, combined with the fact that the discussions were too general in nature. When initially trying to launch these communities, the closer they can be tied to the specific workflow and perceived direct benefits to the performers' performance, the better.

One way to do this is to introduce social learning through project-based communities, rather than those that are simply role based. Project-based communities have a direct tie to specific business outcomes and will help facilitate these projects in a way not often seen in the course of the performers' normal workflow. The project team can use the social learning platforms mentioned above to combine the power of virtual and immediate collaboration with technologies that can host file sharing, versioning, and distributed teams in a unique way. In order for these communities to thrive, it is often helpful to assign certain roles to help facilitate the experience and guarantee constancy. Although it is possible for an individual to play more than one of these roles, it is always beneficial to distribute these responsibilities to increase overall engagement with more people feeling vested in the outcome. It is also easy to overwhelm any one individual resource. A few roles to consider include:

Technical Sponsors

These individuals are responsible for maintaining the technical requirements needed to keep the platform current, easy to navigate, and readily available. They are often found outside of the line of business directly involved in the community itself, but they should have an understanding of the roles and business processes being supported. They are also critical in helping embed the assets and technology into the PS broker framework outlined above. Having someone managing the relationship with IT is critical to these systems' working and remaining vital.

Content Sponsors

These individuals come from within the business unit being supported. They have overall responsibility for keeping the community going at a high level. They should have a strong understanding of the project being facilitated as well as the roles, responsibilities, and expertise of the individuals involved. Although the community at large is responsible for supplying and maintaining the content throughout the life cycle of the project, the content sponsor may be called upon to facilitate certain discussions or segments of the project that may be lacking or drawing low engagement. They may also be asked to help feed some of the initial content needed to get the conversations and workflows started.

Project Segment Sponsors

Although the content sponsors have responsibility for the overall health of the community, there is often a need for project segment sponsors who help maintain specific portions of the project. These individuals would be responsible for guaranteeing the integrity of the content being posted within their segment and helping individuals understand how to engage within their specific portion of the project. They may be asked to maintain specific project deadlines, help guarantee certain deliverables, and facilitate the community's involvement in their portion of the journey.

Maintain a High Level of Community Credibility

In order for a social learning network to thrive, the content and participants involved need to be credible. That's not to say that some of the discussions and content won't wander at times. As is the case in any collaborative environment, there will be times when the ideas and content shared will be incorrect or need to be validated. The key here is facilitating the validation process as quickly and consistently as possible. Creating some type of maintenance strategy can help with this effort. Although a successful social learning community should ideally regulate itself, this behavior can take a fair amount of time to achieve. To help in the initial phases, an organization should put in place processes and standards around sustaining the dialogue until the community can sustain itself. Even after this is achieved, it is good practice to institute some degree of oversight to ensure that these standards are being maintained and kept current. A social learning community has a natural life cycle, and the level of engagement will evolve over time. These standards need to be kept current based on these changes and adapt accordingly. This will require an intentional effort on the part of those who help maintain these standards. Many organizations are creating specific roles with responsibilities across the enterprise and all communities to help maintain a consistent user experience.

Jumpstart the Discussions to Encourage Interaction

Be prepared to seed the initial discussions and use questioning to jumpstart the engagements. In the early adoption stage of a social learning community, participants often feel uncomfortable being the first to add comments and content. A certain level of trust, comfort, and proven value needs to be reached before a critical mass of engagement will be achieved. Even after this tipping point is realized, however, many communities have a greater number of "lurkers"—those who simply read and consume content—than those who will contribute on a regular basis. It is often helpful to jumpstart these engagements by preseeding the discussion with relevant content and asking questions to encourage interaction. Obviously this content needs to be substantive, and the questions posed need to build on that. For this reason, selecting the right author is critical. Enlisting individuals who are credible and respected by their peers as subject-matter experts is the best way to begin this process.

Post the Names of Frequent Contributors

Post the names of those who contribute the best answers and who participate often. Once the level of engagement increases, it is important to encourage and recognize those who are contributing on a regular basis. Posting the names of those who contribute high-quality answers, have the largest followings, and who participate the most can send a positive message to all involved and can encourage others to do the same.

Another powerful way to build momentum is to have some type

of system in place that recognizes, rewards, and ranks this level of participation. Depending on the platform you chose to host the environment, many will allow you to run reports on the number of views, hits, and contributions each posting receives. Many of these systems will allow the other participants to rate the quality of the posting. They will also enable the postings to be sorted or viewed by these rankings. It is also possible to have these rankings dynamically viewed on the landing page, which helps the performers easily find and access the higher-quality interactions while sending a clear message that the environment encourages and rewards high-quality participation.

Another feature many of these systems offer is the ability to subscribe to a highly ranked and applicable posting or all postings by a particular author. This way the performers are proactively notified when there is a change to content they find interesting, and it also lets them know when a particular author adds additional content. Each of these methods encourages the entire learning community to participate and recognize a greater value in the experience and knowledge shared.

Personalize the Social Learning Environment

Allow the experience and environment to be personalized whenever possible. The greatest strength of these communities is the degree to which the content posted and shared can be personalized by individual performers and have a direct impact on their job performance. Few social learning environments survive over the long haul that do not meet this fundamental need.

Many communities permit the environment to be personalized both in experience and in layout. For instance, many of the more popular social learning platforms allow individual performers to create their own landing page or Web page environment. Their site is still linked to the larger community, but it is personalized in such a way that it creates a safe place to invite other participants into a private discussion, to host their own content in a more controlled and safe environment, and to begin to build their own content areas, making the larger collection of data more individual and useful to their specific business needs.

Depending on what the corporate learning culture will allow, these sites can also have their own customized look and feel and share personal information that individual performers control depending their individual security settings. With each level of individualization allowed, the probability of the performers' seeing a more direct and powerful degree of impact increases.

Allow the Community to Have a Life Cycle of Its Own

Like any social setting, these environments have a natural life cycle that needs to be respected and encouraged. Too many of these communities are maintained or pushed to be sustained well beyond their usefulness. This will only devalue the overall experience and burden the performers with sifting through content that is no longer relevant, vibrant, or useful.

A delicate balance needs to be struck, one that recognizes that there is an ebb and flow in any conversation, and, as was stated earlier, it is the responsibility of the both the community and the content sponsor to keep the dialogue engaging and renewed.

It is also important to recognize when a community has run its course and needs to be retired, archived, or changed to meet a new demand and business need. This is not a sign that the old community is "bad" or that it has lost its overall value. Rather, this type of legacy content can be of great value if archived and allowed to be harvested correctly and in other ways. But it is also important to recognize when a conversation or community should be moved to a different level of engagement and accessibility. It is important for the performers to be able to identify and engage in those communities that can add the greatest value and that have moved on to play a different role.

HOW TO MAKE IT WORK FOR YOU: PLAN SOCIAL LEARNING ACROSS THE FIVE MOMENTS OF LEARNING NEED

Another important aspect for helping social learning thrive is the way in which the overall learning culture integrates and promotes these networks. As will be discussed in greater detail in Chapter 8, learning assets such as social learning networks are only as success- ful as the overall learning culture believes them to be and reinforces them as such. If they are not promoted and positioned correctly across all five moments of need, the performers will default back to what they have historically perceived as the easiest and most efficient resources available: their peers.

In the world of support, performers misinterpret the proximity of a learning asset with its effectiveness in serving a particular moment of need. Just because a peer sits in the cubicle or office around the corner, or just because the help desk is programmed into the speed dial, they are not necessarily the most effective learning assets at the time. In fact, we would argue that peers could be the least effective for a number of reasons:

1. Peers could think that they know the most current infor- mation, but in reality they don't.
2. Peers may not offer the most efficient approach to solv- ing the problem. Peers will default to what has worked best for them when trying to solve a similar problem, but this approach may have come from self-discovery, and they may not be aware of other, more efficient methods.
3. When using peers, or even a help desk, to solve a prob- lem, the answer given may not be delivered in an instruc- tional manner. This can result in the answers not being internalized during the interaction. Being given the an- swer in this manner can encourage the performer to re- main dependent on this resource to solve this, and other problems, in the future rather than learning to become more self-reliant.

Table 6.1. The Social Learning Tools Applicable to the Five Moments of Learning Need

Moment of Need	Recommended Assets	Rational
1. When learning New (for the first time)	• Coaching or mentoring programs • Virtual training-coaching platforms • Virtual worlds	These three social learning assets provide a highly structured and instructionally based experience. They can be designed in a linear fashion and can be highly guiding. A facilitator or an SME can be present who is able to remediate and test for understanding.
2. When learning More	• Coaching or mentoring programs • Virtual training-coaching platforms • Virtual worlds • Blogs • Wikis • Social networking platforms	The same rational listed above would apply for the first three assets listed. The last three assets can be useful when the performer has a base knowledge upon which to build. Design considerations will need to be considered to prequalify and broker performers to content that maps to, and extends, the base knowledge in a seamless manner.
3. When trying to Apply	• Coaching or mentoring programs • Online chats • Microblogs • Blogs • Wikis • Social networking platforms	There is typically an immediacy and working context associated with the Apply moment of need. Because of this, each asset listed needs to be embedded in the workflow as best it can. In this case, a coaching or mentoring program takes on more of a reactive nature than the more proactive and structured approach used by the first two assets. The last four assets are useful only if the Apply moment involves a fair amount of time to completion and if they are written in a way that makes them adaptable to the situations.
4. When things Change	• Coaching or mentoring programs • Virtual meeting platforms • Virtual worlds • Social networking platforms • Microblogs	A Change moment is one in which performers need be notified when a change occurs before they attempt to complete a task. All five of these assets need to be in place in order to meet this need. Microblogging can be used proactively to notify an individual or group.
5. When needing to Solve something that has gone wrong	• Coaching or mentoring programs • Online chats • Microblogs	Like the Apply moment, there is an immediacy associated with this final moment of need. Usually in such cases, time is of the essence. These three assets are highly contextual and better suited for remediation than the other assets available.

4. Finally, and most significant, using peers or help desks to solve a problem involves two or more full-time employees' doing one individual's job. If the performer were more self-reliant and had learned to deal with his or her Apply moments through other, more independent resources, such as preexisting content residing in a social learning network, the amount of time gained and moneys saved through not interrupting a peer would be substantial to the organization.

Reversing this learned behavior of support is not easy. It will take a combination of peers and help desks repeatedly reinforcing the use of other resources, by the effectiveness of these other resources, and by the degree to which social learning is seen as helpful across all five moments of need. Table 6.1 examines each need and discusses where best to position the social learning tools outlined above in ways that optimize their strengths.

INSIGHTS FROM A THOUGHT LEADER: Mark Oehlert

Mark Oehlert is a recognized expert, author, and speaker in the fields of innovation, emerging technology, game-based learning, social media, and virtual worlds. He has worked in the learning field for more than 10 years, bringing his unique insight as a trained historian and anthropologist to a range of challenges from Performance Support to mobile computing and learning strategy development. Oehlert served as a learning strategy architect at the global consulting firm of Booz Allen Hamilton, working with a range of clients in formulating enterprisewide learning and technology strategies. He also supported the Advanced Distributed Learning initiative as the deputy director for communications where he acted as the leadership team's primary e-learning research coordinator. Oehler also served as the director of learning innovations at the MASIE Center, a think tank that works with Fortune 500 companies and is focused on the successful identification and implementation of learning strategies and technologies in the corporate space. Oehlert now serves as an innovation evangelist at the Defense Acquisition

University—a U.S. Department of Defense university focused on improving the learning outcomes for over 150,000 acquisition personnel.

The "Three Horsemen" of Social Learning Implementations

A participatory culture is a culture with relatively low barriers to expression and engagement, strong support for creating and sharing, and some type of informal mentorship whereby what is known by the most experienced is passed along to the novices.[1]

I've worked in the e-learning and Performance Support field for over 10 years. This work has included deployment of many enterprisewide systems like LMSs and CRM systems. I am currently enhancing and deploying several social learning systems within the Defense Acquisition University (DAU) sphere. The DAU is an organization of about 600 people supporting a learning audience of between 150,000 to over 2 million government personnel and support contractors. The greatest lesson from these projects, so far, is that social learning and social media require us to address three fundamental human issues: fear, control, and trust. We have, too often, ignored these in other learning contexts, but we can't with social learning. After all, social learning is first and foremost social.

What is more, when addressing fear, control, and trust, you must not only include the people who are going to be using social learning technologies but also the people implementing them and others who may feel threatened by them. That's right: the big obstacle in implementing social learning systems is that people, especially up the chain, can feel threatened by them. That's why Fear, Control, and Trust are the "Three Horsemen" of Social Learning Implementations.

The Challenge of Fear

The most often heard refrains when attempting to implement social learning are: "What if people say bad things in these environments?" and "What if they say secret things?" Valid concerns no doubt, but they are not new concerns. They were around at the beginnings of e-mail and any connection to the Internet. What never really gets fully considered, when these fears arise, is the other side of the coin. What if they don't? What if people find new ways of collaborating? What if the ability to work together raises company morale? Organizations are very good at considering the risks associated with social learning but not always with assessing the opportunity cost.

The Threat of Loss of Control

The idea of control is also usually brought up somewhere in the discussions of starting a social learning program. It is expressed with statements like, "What will happen if we turn all these people loose to create content?" and "What if people need to rely on the content they find on the company site?" Again, look at this from the upside perspective. What if all those people you turn loose, using these fairly inexpensive systems that are pretty easy to use, actually create some amazing content? What if they turn out to be some of your best teachers? Now that's a positive. As you go forward with a social learning implementation, understand that this dynamic can also be threatening. How do you think the people who are currently known as "experts" in your organization feel about allowing the entire community to demonstrate its prowess? How do you think they may feel about someone "out there" being designated an expert by virtue of his or her contribution to the community? You need to be aware of these potential fears that may seem odd to us but may be very real to others.

Lack of Trust

Finally, we should talk about trust. This is one that I find almost ironic. We hire these people. We grant them access to all kinds of proprietary data and company secrets. We pay them a lot of money. Yet we hesitate to grant them access to Twitter or Facebook. Why? Don't we trust them? Or do we really not trust that WE have done the job that we know needs to be done to ensure that they use these systems safely and in ways that increase productivity? Is it them we don't trust or the job that we've done to prepare them?

So fear, control, trust—these are the three big issues. Tackle them and you'll be well on your way to creating a true participatory culture. This is the kind of culture that would seem to value and promote trust among employees and between supervisors, leadership, management, and their people on the front lines executing their direction. Make no mistake, fear, control, and trust are all issues that must be dealt with in order to successfully exploit the rich capabilities that social media offers us.

7

MANAGING DELIVERABLES WITH CONTENT MANAGEMENT PRACTICES

Anticipate the difficult by managing the easy.

—Lao Tzu

A STORY TO GET STARTED:
A TRAIN RIDE EAST, FROM CON

My great grandparents left their small community of Panguitch in southern Utah to travel by train to New York City. They traveled with a group of friends and stopped in Chicago and saw, for the first time, a new-fangled contraption called an automobile. They had read about this new invention, but they now had an opportunity to actually ride in one. When the touring group was back on the train headed further east, they discussed whether the automobile would ever "catch on." The group took a vote, and it was unanimous: every member of the party concluded that the automobile was a fad that could never really work, especially in southern Utah. Here are some of their rationales:

- At that time there were fewer than 50 miles of paved road in all of the United States. Most roads were rugged, and traveling on them in an automobile would have been unpleasant and difficult.

- Horses could go anywhere and didn't need much of a road, if any. You could travel to anywhere on a horse without restriction of needing paved roads.
- Fuel for the machine was hard to come by and expensive. Horses could eat along the way.
- These machines appeared to be unreliable. What would you do if it stopped working in the middle of nowhere?
- They were noisy.
- They were expensive.

But, as you know the automobile did "catch on" and replace horses and buggies. My great grandparent's travel group was wrong and short sighted.

Several years ago, our industry attempted to develop things called *reusable learning objects* (RLOs). For the most part this effort at content management failed. It was costly, and the reuse effort yielded very little advantage. The effort tarnished the good name of content management. And there were some who rejected it because it would never "catch on." But times are changing. The need for single-source publishing and the management of content in organizations today is growing. Ultimately it will be integrated into the work we do, and it will feel as common to our lives as the automobile does today.

WHAT YOU NEED TO KNOW

Read on if you want to learn how content management ultimately supports Performance Support, and how you can begin to embrace helpful content management practices whether or not you are currently ready to purchase and implement the technologies that are making it happen.

Content Should be Free from Proprietary Formats

In 1978, the American National Standards Institute (ANSI) began the pursuit of a standard for information interchange. Their intent was to free computer-generated content from the constraints of proprietary formatting imposed by the software used to create it. In addition, the ANSI wanted the ability to associate descriptive human-legible information about the nature and role of every element in a document. This capability would provide absolute autonomy to what an organization could do with its content.

In 1984, the International Organization for Standardization (ISO) joined the ANSI in its quest. Together, they invited IBM to pull from IBM's shelves a *generalized markup language* they had begun developing in the 1960s. With some adaptations, the result was the 1985 birth of the Standard Generalized Markup Language (SGML).

The adoption of SGML was fueled by the reality that the United States military had announced that it would no longer accept documents in the myriad of proprietary formats emerging at the time. They wanted to be able to do whatever they needed with the content without constraint. And, SGML was more than qualified to meet this need.

But SGML was a programming language. It was no small fete to implement. There was no WYSIWYG authoring capability. Authors had to embed SGML codes into the text they were authoring as they created it. Generally only larger corporations and agencies that produced massive amounts of content could afford to embrace the heavy implementation costs. This fundamental flaw put SGML on a failure path.

In 1992 researchers at the European Laboratory for Particle Physics (known as CERN) unveiled a *simplified hypertext markup language* they called HTML. HTML was a simple SGML application built to satisfy the needs of the emerging Internet and the limited capacity of a "browser" that would interpret and display it. The child (HTML) soon eclipsed its parent (SGML). But, although HTML provided content independence, it lacked the capacity to associate metadata and transform the content into other forms outside of the browser.

There was little to no capacity to adapt content because HTML was not conveying the "descriptive human-legible information about the nature and role of the elements" in that content.

In 1996 the serious limitations of HTML opened the door to the emergence of the eXtensible Markup Language (XML). XML returned the power and extensibility of SGML, but it retained the simplicity of HTML. The World Wide Web Consortium (W3C) formed a team that stripped away all of the nonessential, unused, cryptic parts of SGML. What remained was a lean and mean markup language with only 26 pages of specifications as opposed to the 500+ pages of the SGML specifications! At the same time, all the useful things that SGML had offered could now be done using XML. The promise of total content independence from proprietary formats was a reality again. Organizations could now move their content from application to application and publish it out from a single source into any form it needed.

Earlier in this book we mentioned the accelerating proliferation of information taking place in every organization. This information faces three fundamental threats:

- **Being restricted in its use and ultimate survival because of proprietary formats:** Today, more than ever, content is capital. It can have great value. Not all content falls into this category, but the reservoir of legitimate content capital is growing in organizations. If it isn't managed and kept independent of proprietary application formats, it is in danger of becoming inaccessible as versions of development software change, and unuseful when an organization needs to deploy that content in a form that is incompatible to the content's native format.
- **Becoming lost in the massive sea of content:** Content, in most organizations, is scattered across the organization. And as the amount of content increases, the capacity to find it diminishes. Federated search capabilities (that is, the searching of several databases simultaneously) can help, but it too often it yields so many possible hits that the time required to sort through it all precludes its pursuit.

- **Becoming outdated and dangerous:** As performers face the challenge of change, they need to have confidence that the content they are accessing is current, that they can rely on it to support the work they are called to do. When the reference content and the guiding support isn't current, performance falters. It can even become dangerous to an organization incurring unnecessary costs, liabilities, and inefficiencies. If these problems become systemic, they can threaten the very survival of the organization.

So preserving content capital, maximizing its potential for the organization, strengthening its availability, reducing the redundant efforts to re-create it because of lack of visibility, and keeping it current so that the operations of the organization are current and sound—these reasons and more drive organizations to ultimately invest in content management strategies and their supporting technologies.

In addition, no organization can learn at or above the speed of change without addressing the need for content currency and adaptability. Content needs to be managed so it can be redeployed in whatever form it is needed to meet the minute-to-minute communication, training, and Performance Support needs of the organization.

No training organization that is serious in its intent to support performance at all Five Moments of Learning Need in an ever-changing marketplace can afford to ignore this need to manage its deliverables with content management practices. These practices must have at their foundations content that is free from all proprietary formatting standards. Content must be safely rooted in XML.

Performance Support Ultimately Justifies Single-Source (Multichannel) Publishing

One of the conundrums of supporting performers across the five moments of need is that their successful performance often requires that the same content to be delivered through multiple modalities. This is because performers are doing everything but standing still. They are on the move. And in order to keep support contextual and immediate, the support often merits access to the same PS content via multiple modalities (for example, mobile devices, printed job aids, Internet reference, and e-learning). Also, each of the five moments of need often requires a different modality in support of the same performance.

Here's an example: Table 7.1 shows the rationale for incorporating multiple modalities across the five moments of need for customer service representatives (CSRs) who have a set of software-guided tasks that they complete as they work with customers over the phone. They perform these tasks many times a day every day.

The example in Table 7.1 shows how the same content can be deployed through multiple modalities. The question that needs answering here is: How can an organization provide Performance Support across all those modalities without creating a development and maintenance burden that's greater than the benefits? After all, there are very few, if any, training organizations sitting around with time on their hands and unmarked resources. And frankly, if deploying PS content across multiple modalities were to increase only the development costs, organizations might be able to spring for it all. But the greatest challenge of a fully loaded Performance Support offering is the cost of keeping its content current.

Here's where *single-source publishing* (SSP) earns its keep. SSP consists of practices and technologies that allow an organization to write content once and then publish it in all the different forms (modalities) needed. Since the content is kept in a single source, when it needs maintenance, the changes are made to its source file, and then the updated content is published out to all existing forms. For example, consider the CSR scenario described in Table 7.1. Table 7.2 illustrates how single-source publishing would apply in each of the Five Moments of Learning Need.

In a single-source authoring environment like the one described above and in Tables 7.1 and 7.2, the tasks are *content objects*, and they are authored once and then published out along with other content objects to automatically create the student workbook, e-learning module, and the PS broker with its sidekicks, quick-checks, workaround

Table 7.1. The Rationale for Incorporating Multiple Modalities across the Five Moments of Learning Need for CSRs Who Have a Set of Software-Guided Tasks to Complete

Moment of Need	Context	Modality	In the Form Of
Learn New	When the customer service representatives (CSRs) are first hired, they participate in an intensive five-day training course. One of those days focuses on the daily software tasks they complete as they work with customers over the phone. They review the tasks in their workbook where they make notes on various screens and in different steps as the trainer demonstrates the tasks. The CSRs then complete guided and unguided practice exercises using the sidekicks and quick-checks in the digital broker.	Student workbook and digital broker	Task overview and detailed directions with a guided practice exercise
Learn More	Once CSRs complete their initial training and they begin day-to-day work, time is allocated for them to continue their learning. During these study times, CSRs complete e-learning modules that focus on learning additional software tasks, and they review the core tasks they learned during their instructor-led training (ILT).	E-learning	Review exercise
Apply	At any point when the CSRs are working, they can pull up a task sidekick to follow as they complete a task while working with a customer. And, for the first three months on the job, CSRs complete periodic quick-checks that they initiate themselves based on performance improvement goals they have set with their supervisor.	Digital broker	Sidekick and quick-check (as a checklist)
Adapt to Change	Quarterly, changes are made to the call center software. Two weeks prior to implementing those changes, CSRs attend a virtual Internet briefing on the changes. During the briefing, CSRs receive a paper-based job aid that lists the tasks that have changed, a brief description of the changes, and the control key sequence that will push the appropriate task sidekick and/or quick-check to the CSR. CSRs can opt to post the job aid where they can quickly refer to it during the first few days following the upgrade.	Paper-based job aid and digital broker	Sidekick and quick-check

(continued)

| Solve a Problem | From time to time, a CSR will encounter a customer whose needs can't be resolved by following the remaining steps of a specific customer service task. In such cases, the CSR will take the following steps:
• Access the sidekick for that task (if the CSR hasn't already done so).
• Double click on the step of the task where the remaining steps aren't applicable and enter the workaround section of the PS broker.
• Review the exception policy tied to that task and step.
• Review the approved and rejected workaround notes from other CSRs who have encountered customer challenges at this step of the task.
• Check to see if any of the approved workarounds will work for the customer.
• If not, formulate and enter into the system a "proposed workaround" for the customer.
• The proposed workaround is automatically e-mailed to an available supervisor who reviews it and accepts or rejects it and then pushes the e-mail back to the CSR.
• If rejected, the CSR forwards the call to the supervisor. | PS broker and e-mail | Workaround section in t. PS broker |

sections, and so on. As mentioned, although this delivers a savings in production costs, the real benefit of single-source publishing occurs when content requires changing. In a single-source environment, the author can make the change in the source document and then push the change back out across multiple publishing channels.

Author Your PS Solution with a Structure That Will Ultimately Support It

Whether or not your organization is ready to embrace single-source publishing (SSP), you should begin authoring, sooner rather than later, the content within a structure that will ultimately support it. This is the best first step toward SSP. And even if you don't plan to move to SSP, structured authoring delivers additional benefits

Table 7.2. An Example of How Single-Source Publishing Would Apply in Each of the Five Moments of Learning Need

Learn New	The tasks in the sidekicks and quick-checks are the same content as those in the student workbook. They were published to each of these modalities from a single source.
Learn More	The review exercises are the same content as that used during the ILT. They were published to this e-learning modality from a single source.
Apply	The content in the sidekicks and their associated quick-checks is the same. They were published from a single source.
Adapt to Change	The content in the job aids, sidekicks, and their associated quick-checks is the same. They were published from a single source.
Solve a problem	In this case, the system step appearing in the workaround section of the PS broker is published there from a single source.

by strengthening the usability of your Performance Support solutions.

What is structured authoring? *Structured authoring* takes place whenever content developers author within a consistent set of information structures. These information structures occur at two levels: at the modality level and at the content-type level.

Modality Information Structures

In the performer support arena, a *modality* is the tangible vehicle through which content is made available and operational in the support of performance. Examples of modalities are these:

- Job aids: planners, sidekicks, and quick-checks (published to paper or digitally)
- Student workbooks and facilitators' guides for instructor-led training (published to paper and/or pdf documents)
- E-learning modules or courses

```
Get Started
        Where Am I (Course Map)
Check My Learning Goals
        Take a Quick Start (20 Minute Path)
Learn About
        Concept 1
        Concept 2
Learn How To
        Task 1
        Task 2
Practice
        Increase My Understanding (Concept Practice Games)
        Build My Skills (Task Integration Activities in the Form of Unguided Practice
        Scenarios)
Apply
        Make a Plan
        Select Job Aids
Explore Further
        Access Related Modules and/or Courses
        Expand My Understanding
        Connect and Learn with Others
```

Figure 7.1. An Example of an Information Structure That Could Be Imposed across an E-Learning Modality

- Digital Performance Support brokers
- Online help
- Internet reference system

Figure 7.1 provides an example of an information structure that could be imposed across an e-learning modality.

In the example in Figure 7.1, structured authoring dictates that every e-learning module be organized according to this structure. Learners would see these labels in the learning menu of every module. E-learning developers would author the e-learning content according to this structure.

Content-Type Objects and Content-Type Structures

If the e-learning structure described above were part of a single-source authoring system, the module would be automatically populated by instances of content-type objects. For example, the "Learn How To" section would be populated with a unique type of content called *tasks*. The "Learn About" section of the e-learning module would be populated with a unique type of content called *concepts*. The "Practice" section calls for a unique type of content called *unguided practice scenarios*.

These three content types are very different in nature. When you set them next to each other, they look different and they have very different intents and functions. A *concept* is something you understand, and a *task* is something you do. A task differs from an unguided practice scenario in form and purpose. A task has a set of steps that systematically walk the performer through a set of actions that accomplish a specific outcome. An *unguided practice scenario* doesn't describe the steps for accomplishing an outcome. It provides a learner with a scenario and then invites the learner to respond to the scenario. It may or may not indicate which task or set of tasks the learner should perform. The *course map* is another content type. The *practice games* for concepts is still another.

Here is where structured authoring pays off. In a student workbook, the core chapter structure has the same content-type objects as the e-learning module (for example, task objects, concept objects, and unguided practice scenarios). And as long as these content objects are structured so they can function in both modalities, you have the capacity to automatically populate predefined modality structures (in this case an e-learning module and a student workbook) with content written following the unique structure for each content type. Figure 7.2 provides an example of the content-type structure for a reusable task object.

This kind of structured authoring has many benefits beyond that of making single-source publishing possible. Imposing a consistent content structure is one of the most powerful organization guidelines you can follow. An information structure accomplishes the following:

- **Provides a consistent performer interface:** When performers access content that has a consistent information structure, they navigate through that content with greater comfort and

Task Name
Context Statement

Step	Action	Response	Comments
1			Step guidelines
			Decision support commentary
			Detailed practice scenario
			Concept bridges
			References

Related Tasks
Related Concepts

Figure 7.2. An Example of the Content-Type Structure for a Reusable Task Object

efficiency because they understand the structure. There are no surprises. They can scan through the content and focus on the content immediately rather than spending time trying to figure out how it is organized. This is especially true as the amount of content increases in volume. The content that is consistently structured becomes more navigable, intuitive, and useful.

- **Enhances readers' ability to remember the content:** A consistent structure can decrease the time it takes to encode information into long-term memory and facilitate the speed and ease with which it is retrieved from long-term memory. In other words, performers learn faster and remember better.

- **Accommodates learning dispositions and reference requirements:** Regardless of readers' disposition toward learning, they can use the structure to their advantage. For example, *transforming learners* can skip introductory material and go directly to the content they need. *Conforming learners* can choose to move through the content sequentially, taking advantage of the structure to reinforce their learning confidence.

- **Reduces development and maintenance time:** A consistent content structure allows you to boilerplate. Once you have developed one module, chapter, or job aid, you can strip from it the unique content and use the skeleton structure for the remaining modules, chapters, or job aids. Also, you can separate stable content from dynamic content, and write all of the stable content objects ahead of the unstable. Generally, concept objects are more stable than task objects.

Here's the point: Regardless of the benefits of single-source publishing, structured authoring merits implementation as part of any performer support strategy for the very benefits listed above. And when the time comes for your organization to embrace SSP, the more content you have in place with consistent information structures, the better off you will be. You will be up and running more readily. The cost to implement SSP will be significantly less.

HOW TO MAKE THIS WORK FOR YOU: DEFINE YOUR CONTENT STRUCTURES

Here is the process for defining your content structures:

1. Conduct Learning Asset Analysis

You can find the instructions for conducting learning asset analysis in Chapter 5. What you need to understand here is the reason why you want to follow the learning asset analysis at this point in the process. Earlier in this chapter, in the discussion of structured authoring, we described a modality as "the tangible vehicle through which content is made available and operational in the support of performance." When you conduct learning asset analysis, you examine all the forms of the different modalities you are employing in supporting learners at all Five Moments of Learning Need. During that assessment you get rid of some, consolidate and/or modify others, and add any that are missing. Table 7.3 is an example of what the results of this analysis might look like.

Table 7.3. An Example of a Learning Asset Analysis

Type of Modality / Learning Asset	Learn New	Learn More	Apply	Adapt to Change	Solve a Problem
Digital Performance Support Broker	✓	✓	✓	✓	✓
Student Workbook and Facilitators Guide	✓	✓			
eLearning Course	✓	✓			
eLearning Bursts			✓	✓	✓
Job Aids: planners, sidekicks, and quick-checks	✓	✓	✓	✓	✓
Mobile Support			✓	✓	✓

If Table 7.3 were the end result of your learning asset analysis, each one of these designations would be an asset type for which you would want to define an information structure.

2. Define a Structure for Each Type of Asset

In this second phase, you define the information structure for each asset. For example, in the list of modality types in Table 7.3, one of the assets is a student workbook. Figure 7.3 provides an example of a possible information structure it might employ. In this case every workbook would have this same structure.

Note that there is a pattern in this example where structure is imposed at every level of the asset. The structure on the left in Figure 7.3 is the structure for the workbook. The next level is the core chapter structure shown on the right. Every chapter in the workbook would have the five sections shown. Content authors would create

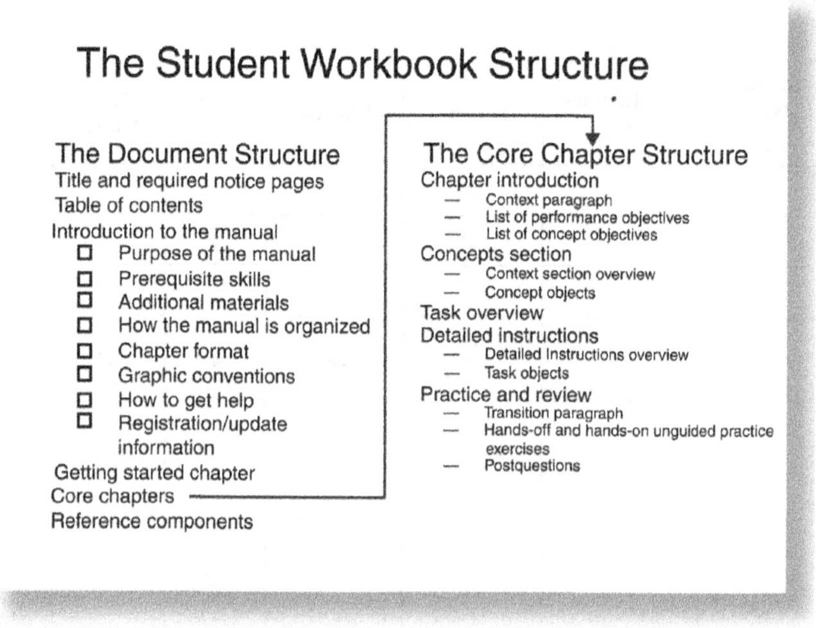

The Student Workbook Structure

The Document Structure
Title and required notice pages
Table of contents
Introduction to the manual
- ☐ Purpose of the manual
- ☐ Prerequisite skills
- ☐ Additional materials
- ☐ How the manual is organized
- ☐ Chapter format
- ☐ Graphic conventions
- ☐ How to get help
- ☐ Registration/update information

Getting started chapter
Core chapters
Reference components

The Core Chapter Structure
Chapter introduction
- — Context paragraph
- — List of performance objectives
- — List of concept objectives

Concepts section
- — Context section overview
- — Concept objects

Task overview
Detailed instructions
- — Detailed Instructions overview
- — Task objects

Practice and review
- — Transition paragraph
- — Hands-off and hands-on unguided practice exercises
- — Postquestions

Figure 7.3. An Example of a Possible Information Structure for a Student Workbook

content within these structures. And even the content areas underneath the five sections would have consistent structures as well. But these have a unique role to play, that of content-type objects.

3. Identify the Content Types

Once you have established structures for each type of modality, you analyze the structures to look for the different types of content that populate each of the information structures. Content types can include system tasks, concepts, policies, practice exercises, business process flows, system message explanations and solutions, report and/or form descriptions, and definitions of terms.

Once you have identified all the unique types of content for each of the modalities, you then compare them across the assets to determine where there are common content types. Table 7.4 shows how the various types of content relate to each of the modality (asset)

Table 7.4. An Example of a Comparison of the Types of Content for Each of the Modalities to the Types of Learning Assets

Content Types	PS Broker	Student Work-book	E-Learn-ing	E-Burst	Planner	Side-kick	Quick-Check	Mobile Support
Tasks	✓	✓	✓	✓	✓	✓	✓	✓
Concepts	✓	✓	✓	✓	✓	✓	✓	✓
Policies	✓							
Practice scenarios	✓	✓	✓	✓	✓	✓	✓	✓
Business process flows	✓	✓	✓					✓
System message solutions	✓					✓		✓
Report and/ or form descriptions	✓				✓	✓		
Definitions of terms	✓	✓	✓	✓	✓	✓	✓	✓

types. These content types (on the left) can become interchangeable building blocks for the assets (listed across the top) as long as they have a common information structure that satisfies the instructional needs of each asset.

4. Define the Content Type Structures

An overall component structure is created by identifying standard headings for the content object. These headings define the structure. The value of doing this was discussed earlier in this chapter. Table 7.5 is an example of a specific instance for a "Job Aid Object." In this case, the content structure was imposed upon every

Table 7.5. An Example of a Specific Instance for a Job Aid Object

CRAY JCL Statement: ACQUIRE	
Statement Form:	ACQUIRE, DN=dn, PDN=pdn, MF=MS,ID=id,^R-rdpass, UQ,TEXT='txtstring'
Description:	This COS JCL statement makes a dataset permanent on the Cray disks and local to the job. If the dataset does not reside on the Cray disks, it is staged from the mainframe specified by the MF parameter. See Chapter 6, "Building the Job Control Language," for additional information on this command.
Simple Example: *(Required parameters only)*	*acquire,dn=mydata,mf=ms,text="flnm=/smi th/di rname/afile'.*
Complex Example: *(Optional and Required Parameters)*	*acquire,dn=mydata, mf=ms, id=smi th, w=wpasswd, r=rpass^ wd,* *uq, text="user=jones,mvn=ct9999^* *noaccnt,flnm="model/run1/ dataother',maxerr=3'.*

Parameter Definitions:	**DN=DN** *Required:* Replace "dn" with the local dataset name
	 PDN=pdn Optional: Replace "pdn" with the permanent dataset name.
	    • If you specify this parameter, you cannot specify the FLNM parameter.
	    • If you do not specify the PDN, the DN is used as the PDN.

Cray JCL Statement. The entire set of these objects was intended to support the performers' use of the Cray Computer Job Control Language.

The intent here is *not* for you to understand what a job control language (JCL) statement is. What we want you to see is the left-hand structure. If there were 200 JCL statements, every one would have the components listed down the left. These headings would not change, and the order for the headings would remain constant, thereby establishing a consistent information structure.

5. Assign Content Stewards to Facilitate Collaborative Development

Collaborative development is the most efficient development solution to structured authoring. *Collaborative development* requires the identification of content stewards, the establishment of their specific roles and responsibilities, and the development of an infrastructure to support content stewards in their various roles and responsibilities.

Here's how you go about it.

Step 1. Identify content stewards, and establish their roles and responsibilities.

A *content steward* is a person who has a particular role and responsibility vis-à-vis specific content. For example, if the specific content were step-by-step instructions for system tasks, you might have four content stewards: a technical writer, a trainer, a technology specialist, and a business specialist. These stewards would have differing roles and responsibilities for the development and maintenance of this specific content. The technical writer would have the responsibility to actually write and update this content including creating screen captures. The trainer would have the responsibilities of providing practice scenarios and adding comments. The technology specialist would have the responsibility of ensuring that the steps were technically accurate and also notifying the other stewards of any changes in the technology. The business specialist would have the responsibility of ensuring that the practice scenarios were relevant to the mission and vision of the organization. This specialist would also contribute comments at appropriate steps regarding the business application of the technology. Successful collaborative development requires that one person assume responsibility for overall management of the content.

Step 2. Develop an infrastructure to support content stewards.

A support infrastructure can help ensure that a cohesive development process exists within which the content stewards can work together effectively. A support infrastructure can include development templates, checklists, project management tools, and direct automated feedback from reviewers, training and support services personnel, and end users.

INSIGHTS FROM A THOUGHT LEADER: Bryan Chapman

Bryan Chapman is the chief learning strategist at Chapman Alliance, a provider of research-centric consulting solutions that assist organizations to define, operate, and optimize their strategic learning initiatives. As a veteran in the industry, he has over 20 years' experience, and he has worked with such organizations as American Express, Shell, Kodak, Sprint, Sharp Electronics, Honda, IBM, Microsoft, Avon, UNICEF, the U.S. Food and Drug Administration, and the U.S. State Department to help them optimize learning efficiency through the use of innovative learning techniques and technologies.

Chapman was formerly the director of research and strategy for independent research and consulting firm Brandon Hall Research, where he served as the primary author and researcher on high-profile projects such as the LMS Knowledgebase, the LCMS Comparative Analysis Report, Comparison of Simulation Products and Services, and a comprehensive study of custom content developers in the industry. In addition, Chapman was responsible for structuring Brandon Hall Research's consulting practice. He continues to provide technology selection services in partnership with Brandon Hall Research as a registered asssociate.

Reusability 2.0: The Key to Publishing Learning

Source: http://www.xyleme.com/resource_library#White papers

Reuse of learning content has had a major impact on organizations that have been transformed from a "training" to a "learning" environment and the way they leverage learning technologies to align with business and educational needs. It wasn't always that way. In the early days of computer-based training (CBT), courses were crafted as large, monolithic structures, several hours in length. Learners traversed a designated path through learning events, in the exact sequence prescribed by a course designer. This worked well for specific, high-profile learning initiatives, delivered via one medium and designed to reach very large target audiences. But it was also extremely cost prohibitive for most, it required lengthy development cycles, and it caused an unmanageable quagmire when it came to updating training.

Around the beginning of the year 2000, commercial learning content management systems (LCMSs) introduced the concept of "learning objects" and the ability to reuse content across multiple courses. We learned how to create smaller, bite-sized modules as a team as opposed to working individually to author courses. The most important lesson we learned from early reusability attempts (reusability 1.0) was that modularization of learning content enables us to create derivative versions of courses for different audiences and even to reuse digital media assets (such as graphics, video, and animations) in other courses. For the most part, the technology works well to streamline development and to update content; however, most of these lessons have been applied only to the production of singular or limited delivery formats such as e-learning and Performance Support, ignoring the fact that classroom, print-based, and face-to-face interaction are still the most pervasive forms of learning we use today and that they will remain in place as long as there are people involved in the learning process.

So the problem is this: How do we get our arms around the bigger picture and fully embrace all formats of learning delivery, across the board? How do we (1) decrease the cost of learning development, (2) reduce lengthy development cycles, and (3) create an environment in which content changes are made instantaneously, across all learning delivery formats?

The answer is reusability 2.0.

Reusability 2.0 Defined

Reusability 2.0 doesn't detract from any of the benefits of current reusability practices. Rather, it adds further dimension and reach to what's possible in supporting all methods of learning delivery across the entire organization. Consider the following definition:

Definition

> **Reusability** 2.0: A method of creating, organizing, storing, versioning, and publishing reusable learning content in a common, central repository for the purpose of creating learning support, *regardless of delivery format* (that is, instructor guides, lesson plans, classroom visuals, tests, handouts, online courses, and job aids).

Another way to look at reusability 2.0 is to compare and contrast it with other modes of learning development. Figure 7.4 classifies production methods used to create a wide array of many different formats of instructional delivery. Each numbered zone on the chart represents an approach to production.

For example, in zone 1, a development team creates content for a specific learning purpose, using traditional authoring or other content development tools. Again, this was the technique used to create full CBT courses in the early days, and it is still frequently used by many organizations, even as courses become more modular by design.

Zone 2 illustrates the methodology used by most organizations today—namely, to use multiple tools, each of which is designed to use its specific nature to create learning content, such as using Microsoft Word to create a lesson plan, PowerPoint to create class visuals, and authoring tools to create online courses.

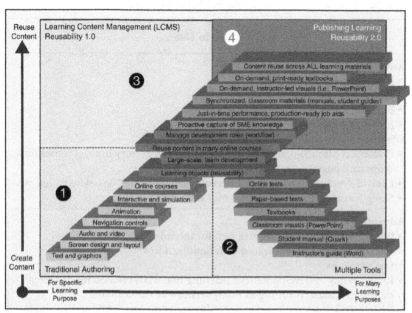

Figure 7.4. Production Methodologies Used to Create Learning Content
Source: Bryan Chapman

In zone 3, the development groups leverage the principles of modular content, team development, and reusing content for specific or limited-use delivery formats. LCMS technology is one of the main methods to support content reuse for specific learning purposes.

Zone 4 utilizes reusability 2.0 practices to structure content in such a way that it supports the widest possible range of learning materials and interventions through a single-pass production, resulting in automatic synchronization of the content across all delivery formats. Table 7.6 outlines the advantages and disadvantages of each methodology.

Case Studies

Reusability 2.0 holds the keys for moving toward a publishing model of learning, as illustrated by the following case studies. The first two case studies focus on organizations that were already in the publishing business, long before encountering reusability 2.0 technologies. The case studies describe how they made the migration toward full reusability and the results of their transformation. Publishers have long understood the efficiencies of using a systematic production model to create products. It is no wonder that publishers would be some of the first to apply emerging technology to (1) reduce the development costs, (2) decrease the length

Table 7.6. Advantages and Disadvantages of Different Development Methodologies

Zone	Production Methods	When to Use
1	Create content for a specific learning purpose, using traditional authoring tools (i.e., Flash, Dreamweaver, Articulate, Lectora Publisher, ToolBook, etc.).	**Advantages** • Highly interactive • Rich screen layout and design • Portable and self-contained • Low-cost tools **Disadvantages** • Content is often siloed on individual computers—very limited reusability (copy and paste) • Lack of synchronization with instructor-led and print-based learning, etc. • Steep learning curves to master tool sets
2	Create content for many learning purposes using multiple tools (i.e., Word, FrameMaker, PowerPoint, multimedia authoring tools, etc.).	**Advantages** • Best-of-breed tools are feature rich for intended purposes • Content creators like working with familiar tools **Disadvantages** • Redundancy in development of learning materials created for different delivery formats, resulting in many versions of the content • Different skill set required to use different tools (not working in a single application) • Difficulties integrating output from different tools • Changes require many modifications and in multiple files
3	Reuse content for specific learning purposes, using learning content management systems (LCMS or proprietary, in-house tools). Reusability 1.0	**Advantages** • Content can be reused across multiple courses • Content is centrally located, organized, and deployed • Changes can be made across multiple courses • Derivative courses can be created for many different audiences **Disadvantages** • Some systems have "plumbing" for reuse across many delivery types, but they lack tools to automatically output to print-ready, formatted learning materials, such as lesson manuals, student guides, job aids, textbooks, and other forms of delivery
4	Reuse content for many learning purposes beyond e-learning, using tools that incorporate reusability 2.0 characteristics. Reusability 2.0	**Advantages** • Single-pass production results in automatic synchronization of output to print-ready, formatted learning materials, such as lesson manuals, student guides, job aids, textbooks, and other forms of delivery • Future proofing content by keeping it all centrally located • Changes to content need to be made only once • On-demand customization of content can be achieved across all output types **Disadvantages** • Requires structure and discipline to achieve full synchronization across all output formats (change management)

Source: Bryan Chapman

of production time, (3) simplify the process of updating content, and (4) in so doing, create a brand-new type of product offering, allowing end-user customers to create and customize their own learning experience.

Case study 3 looks at how the same principles of reusability and production techniques can be applied to the learning and business requirements of one of the world's largest retailers and how the company achieved the same benefits experienced by publishers in supporting a broad-based training effort.

We would like to thank Xyleme for being a sponsor for this research and for introducing us to key stakeholders in each of the case study organizations. We recognize that there are many organizations out there applying reusability 2.0 techniques and that reusability is not exclusive to Xyleme. It was truly a learning experience to get to know and research the transformation that occurred in each situation. There are many great lessons to be learned by examining these transformations. Enjoy.

CASE STUDY #1
Vertical Market, Learning Services, and Information Publisher

Company Profile

This information publisher literally dominates its specialized, technical skills market. In fact, over 80 percent of professionals in this vertical industry, across the world, use at least some of the company's information and/or learning services. In addition to its textbook line, the company produces and sells training resources (such as lesson plans and student guides) to thousands of partners and schools around the globe. Their training materials are also delivered as packaged solutions with the primary equipment used regularly by professionals.

Challenges

One of the main challenges facing this publishing company was to reach a new generation of younger, Web-savvy learners, looking to access personalized training on demand, adapted for their own specialized needs. Prior to embracing reusability 2.0, the company had already established a successful series of computer-based training (CBT) products in tandem with its textbook line, providing versions of its content as self-paced learning modules (built as comprehensive courses with limited reusability across delivery formats). Making the transition to a new paradigm would require that the CBT business remain a priority while achieving better alignment across the production of other support materials.

Previous Methods of Development

The publisher had been working toward single-source publishing for several years before making the full jump to reusability 2.0. The development team used FrameMaker as a data source to create instructors' guides and student manuals. Although CBT development did leverage content contained in FrameMaker, at some point in the process, content had to be transferred from FrameMaker into storyboards and subsequently into multimedia authoring tools; in effect, the company needed to create new versions of content, each requiring its own update and review cycle. The problem was compounded by the fact that all course materials—whether CBT, instructors' guides, manuals, text, or something else—needed to be adapted for professional certification, using different equipment, creating even more versions of the content. Eventually, the process became virtually unmanageable without applying substantial resources to customize learning for each configuration and branding training for partners.

The project manager told us, "There were actually many attempts to single-source content and to find the best solutions. In the end, there were as many solutions as there were people."

Solution

"Our primary goal in moving in this direction [reusability 2.0] was to strategically find a better way to simultaneously develop multiple learning-delivery formats in support of the needs of our target audience and the way they want to learn," said a manager of the process. "Our vision is to base all our learning solutions on single source of content, rather than develop products in isolation. Even more importantly, by single-sourcing content development, we can deliver learning based on specific learner profiles that change based on their own situations and equipment configuration."

The solution was to convert 700 pages of textbook content (from several textbooks) into a central, XML-based, reusable-object repository (Xyleme LCMS) and structure learning content so it would feed all target delivery formats from a single SCO (SCORM Content Object), including (1) CBT; (2) classroom manuals, containing instructors' guides and student manuals; (3) postcourse, just-in-time Performance Support modules, accessible online; (4) paper-based exams used for certification; and (5) providing a new method for creating custom versions of the textbook materials through on-demand printing.

Tactical Approach

The publisher decided to apply reusability 2.0 to its highest-profile, flagship product line before applying the process to other mainstream products. The main product is a comprehensive course that prepares learners to obtain a professional license. "Each content area is assigned to a 'triad'—a group of three developers including a subject-matter expert (SME), an instructional designer, and a technical writer. In total we will have eight triads working across the entire curriculum. Each team works to update existing textbook content and structure the information to best support all target delivery formats. The role of the SME on the team is to revalidate content to match advancements in technology and advancements in understanding new processes and procedures in each discipline area."

Textbooks for the course are currently rich with graphics and illustrations that work to the advantage of the developers. For example, as new graphics are produced, they are stored in a central digital asset repository in 72-dpi, 300-dpi, and 600-dpi formats in support of synchronizing all delivery outputs. "The system is intelligent enough to pull the right graphic for each delivery type. It uses 600 dpi for print materials and 72 dpi for CBT and just-in-time learning." In addition, interactive learning activities are created specifically for output to CBT, yet stored in the same content repository. "When designing for different outputs, our designers simply tag the right media to match the output type. If we need to make changes to the content, whether a graphic or interaction, all the content is found in the same place for ease of update."

Business Drivers and Results

One of the primary drivers in making the shift is to decrease the expense and complexity in creating on-demand products for customers. Although the project is still in the early phases of implementation, they are already experiencing the benefits of systematically updating the text as a single-source feed for all development in support of on-demand, customizable learning products that can be used for many purposes. Another, equally important aspect of the project is to continually keep source content as current as possible. According to the project manager, "We've been in business for 70 years. We have a state-of-the-art printing facility right here on site. The new process will give us the opportunity to do something we haven't been able to do well in the past—that is, to make changes to the content that will immediately update and synchronize all our product offerings from classroom materials to textbooks and in our CBT courses. The impact of this should not be underestimated."

Certification Preparation and Educational Learning Provider: WestNet Learning

Company Profile

WestNet Learning provides information technology courses and learning materials to corporations, educational institutions, training centers, and individuals. Over 1,000 community colleges, universities, high schools, and other academic organizations use their dynamically scalable content. In addition, companies like Cisco and Avaya use WestNet materials to train their own internal employees and partners worldwide. They offer certification preparation in many key topic areas including 3Com, Novell, CompTIA, NACSE, Avaya, Cisco, and Microsoft.

Challenges

"We're a little different than others in the space. We've been on the path to create single-source content for 10 years now. In the early days, we created many of our own technology platforms for reusability. For a number of years we simultaneously did software development to build reusable content repositories AND developed our own content. We came to the realization that our expertise is in content development, content delivery, managing the process, and integrating learning systems. It is not in developing software applications."The biggest challenge is that the company, from the very beginning, has provided many different types of learning outputs including manuals, study guides, Web courses, and self-prep exams. Managing content for all delivery types from a single production pass has been difficult.

Another significant challenge has been coordinating content from hundreds of subject-matter experts, who live across the globe.

Previous Methods of Development

"In our previous development cycles, we would develop a textbook or study guide in Frame-Maker. Information was manually extracted to build courses in HTML. We had other developers who would manually create PowerPoint slides for use in classrooms, as well as tests, student guides, and instructor manuals. Each product was manually built, increasing the cost of course development. Consequently, we couldn't keep the cost down so that our products would be affordable enough for colleges, universities, high schools, or small- to medium-sized companies because the cost of production and customization was just too far out of reach.

"We also have tried several commercial LCMS products, many of which were on the right trail to single-pass production. When investigating solutions, we discovered that many of the systems claim to support multiple output formats, but when you actually pull back the covers, you find that it certainly isn't seamless."

Solution

The solution was (a) to migrate and parse reusable content objects, contained in 300 course modules, each module being anywhere from one to two hours in length, into XML using Xyleme LCMS, and (2) to provide access to hundreds of content contributors, including SMEs world-wide.

Tactical Approach

Here's how the process works when creating a new course. First, a project lead creates a design document and a taxonomy (master table of contents) of all topics to be included in the course. Once the topic areas have been validated, sections are assigned to appropriate subject-matter experts, regardless of where they live. WestNet uses Xyleme's SME Forms feature to collect information directly from subject-matter experts, who are typically high-level, master instructors in their area of expertise, including writing content, objectives, procedures, test questions, and adding instructors' notes. Because all information is directly fed into the XML database, the next step is for the project manager to review the content and prepare it for publishing. Editors also work on the material for clarity, consistency, and grammatical errors. During this phase, graphic artists and animators can also work on visual media to be used in printed materials and inside e-courses.

"We discovered that one person is able to coordinate and manage the entire process, which might have a dozen SMEs working on a particular project. The end result is that following data collection and through a single production pass, we automatically generate all these outputs including a study guide, e-course modules, paper test, Web test, PowerPoint for the classroom, and everything else."

Business Drivers and Results

The company has a vision and goal to (1) dramatically reduce the time it takes to create content, by (2) eliminating redundancy from content gathering, through production, to creating learning products.

Using previous, manual production techniques, it often took between 12 and 18 months to develop all the learning materials associated with a course from date of concept to final release. The result of applying reusability 2.0 is that the process is now compressed to only a few months of development, most of which is spent facilitating data collection.

Another important goal was to simplify the process of systematically upgrading and making changes to the content.

"The beauty of this approach is that we can go in and change a module, and then redeploy the whole package, and the changes will appear in all the different learning formats. We don't have to go in manually and change every little thing. We were not able to do that with traditional desktop authoring tools."

The most important goal of the project was to allow end-user customers the ability to build their own courses by designating specific learning outcomes. WestNet customers purchase subscriptions to the content, and with the subscription comes the ability to create course materials on the fly.

"Our customers can pick from a list of outcomes and click the Go button. Behind the scenes, a custom course is automatically created with all the desired outputs from instructor-led materials, to e-courses, to practice tests."

CASE STUDY #3

Large Corporate: Yum Brands (KFC, Taco Bell, Pizza Hut, and More)

Company Profile

Yum Brands, Inc., is one of the world's largest restaurant companies with 34,000 restaurants in 106 countries and 900,000 employees. You may recognize their popular brands including KFC, Taco Bell, Pizza Hut, Long John Silver's, and A&W, to name a few. To understand the size and scale of this operation, consider the fact that they open three new restaurants every day, each year.

Challenges

From a training perspective, the company has a unique set of challenges including (1) delivering consistent, standard-based training to 900,000 employees in 30 different languages; (2) creating derivatives versions of learning content to match brand, equipment configuration, special needs, and so on, for each of 34,000 locations, many of which are owned by franchise owners; and (3) providing cost-effective methods for delivering customized content to restaurants that average between 30 and 35 employees per location.

Previous Methods of Development

"At the center, our focus is on creating standard guides, which are like standard operations manuals. Inside the manual are all the procedures on how to create products, operate human resources at the restaurant level, and manage the restaurant—basically everything you need to know to run a restaurant according to a brand standard. The problem was that restaurants require variations in the standards to meet local needs such as variances in regional HR practices, different equipment used to create product, and different languages."

Using a traditional training model, local owners would use standard operating manuals as their sources for creating on-site training, whether accomplished in a classroom or taught individually, depending on the size and need of each restaurant. From the source material, they created instructor-led training materials, new hire orientations, job aids, observation checklists, and any other training materials they needed.

This resulted in many different versions of operating manuals and related training materials. To compound the problem further, it was becoming increasingly difficult to manage the versions, and much of the content was siloed on individual computers and siloed within individual business units.

To illustrate the point, when a content audit was done across a number of topic areas, the team identified multiple different, documented procedures to perform the same task. All of the procedures were within safety guidelines and had only minor variances in the process; yet it caused confusion in the restaurant about which procedural task was the "right" one to follow. This led the group to rethink the process for (1) publishing standards, (2) making learning materials more consistent to match brand standards, and (3) synchronizing content across all delivery formats.

Solution

The solution was to migrate approximately 300 word documents that fill seven large binders into a central repository for the purpose of synchronizing content across all delivery formats including a consistent master resource for creating their operating standards library; master files that can be generated into customized operations manuals, taking regional variables (such as local laws and local product offerings) into account; print-ready job aids that can be generated from customized operational manuals, laminated and placed at the point of performance; and finally observation checklists used by supervisors and regional managers to evaluate employee performance. Xyleme LCMS was selected to meet this challenge.

Tactical Approach

A large international region was selected for initial implementation, representing 400 restaurants. The first area of focus was to migrate and synthesize a master standards library as a corporate baseline from which derivative versions could be localized for regional use—basically pulling in the content of all seven binders into an XML database.

Next, in order to synchronize delivery output into all target formats, many of the observation checklists had to be rewritten in procedural format, rather than in question format, to completely align operations manuals with performance appraisals and job aids. For example, instead of saying, "Did the employee wash hands after touching unprepared food?" the evaluation statement was simply changed to, "The employee washed hands after touching unprepared food." The result was that the system immediately generated production-ready, illustrated job aids that matched training requirements and observation checklists that align completely with operation manuals.

Content developers tag content with specific variables that allow local franchises to literally create their own operating manuals on demand by selecting the brand, type of equipment, regional considerations, language, and other factors. Based on their selection, Xyleme automatically generates for the new operations manual a customized table of contents as well as automatically generating numbering, headers, and footers. In short, Xyleme creates a complete operational manual for a specific brand restraint that completely matches the restaurant's configuration and culture.

Yum is in the early stages of approaching this new paradigm, and it plans to take a phased approach. During initial implementation, local franchise and regional owners will still create their own training materials from standard operations manuals; however, the big changes will include a view into the various brand and business unit operations manuals that can provide a consistent corporate baseline, upon which most operational training can take place.

Business Drivers and Results

The business drivers that led Yum to consider reusability 2.0, and the metrics that will be used to judge overall success of the project, include the following:

1. Cost reduction
2. Self-serve, on-demand personalization of learning content across all delivery formats
3. Speed of development
4. Ease of content maintenance

5. Widespread adoption beyond the first phases of implementation
6. Ultimately, the streamlining of the number of redundant procedures associated with performing the same task

Early reactions have been very good. Users are impressed by the ability to create customized operations manuals based on corporate brand standards, job aids, and observation checklists. One snag in the road is that some areas still have real issues with access to reliable, persistent Internet connectivity. But in these areas, customized materials can still be created based on regional variations and supplied through traditional channels, such as mailed hardcopy documents or CD-based versions, until connectivity issues can be solved.

In short, local restaurant owners or trainers can access the site on which they can use a simple wizard to quickly generate their own complete set of up-to-date source materials at any time. And at a corporate level, there can be much greater insight into the variances created at the local level. This will ultimately make a world of difference.

"Our perspective is that reusability 2.0 is now emerging as a viable way to address some real business issues. The timing of new technology in the space and our growing needs is just right. If we had tried to solve this problem earlier, it would have been much more difficult, and it would have taken us down a completely different path."

Summary

Reusability 2.0 is not for everyone, nor is it for every training situation. If you are designing a learning intervention that can be readily delivered using a singular delivery format, without many variations, applying this methodology would be overkill. However, if your vision is to systematically synchronize content across all delivery formats and/or you need training to be highly adapted for different learning environments, then reusability 2.0 is your key to publishing learning.

8

IMPLEMENTING YOUR PERFORMANCE SUPPORT STRATEGY

Strategy is: A style of thinking, a conscious and deliberate process, an intensive implementation system, the science of insuring future success.

—*Pete Johnson*

A STORY TO GET STARTED:
TEACHING A CALF TO DRINK FROM A BUCKET, FROM CON

Early life on a dairy farm in southern Utah included the responsibility of teaching new-born calves how to drink from a bucket. The challenge of this chore is that simply placing a bucket of milk down in front of a calf doesn't work. It has no idea how to drink from it. A calf instinctively seeks milk from its mother, and that milk is packaged in nothing that resembles a bucket, and it is oriented in the exact opposite direction. Simply pushing the calf's nose in the milk doesn't work. It will resist with all its strength. Drinking from a bucket is simply contrary to its nature.

But that nature can be changed. A calf needs to be introduced to this new approach in a gradual and familiar way. Here's how you do it. Dip a cupped hand into the bucket so it is full of milk; then allow the calf to begin sucking on the two middle fingers while dribbling the milk from the cupped part of the hand into the mouth. As the calf sucks the fingers, gradually redirect its nose with your other hand down into the bucket of milk. Once its nose enters the bucket of milk, the calf will begin drinking from the milk. Then you slowly remove the hand while the calf continues drinking on its own. This process typically takes a number of attempts until the calf acclimates to the bucket and its disposition to seek milk upwardly is overridden by a new way.

Introducing Performance Support into an already established learning culture needs the same degree of attention. Just like the calf, performers need help unlearning and relearning. Even though Performance Support may be a better and more efficient way to support performers during their Five Moments of Learning Need, it isn't a given that they will automatically embrace it. We have seen stellar Performance Support solutions fail because the implementation strategy was flawed. Since these assets live in the context of the performer's work environment, learning organizations too often assume that performers will naturally see their value and adapt their behavior accordingly. It's sort of like putting a bucket in front of a calf assuming that it will naturally want to drink from it because the calf can get more milk faster.

If you wish to successfully introduce an effective and sustainable Performance Support strategy, you will need to have a well-thought-out implementation plan that takes into account all of the critical variables involved. This chapter will address those issues.

WHAT YOU NEED TO KNOW

Yogi Berra once said, "We're lost, but we're making good time!" It's amazing the number of learning organizations we have worked with that, knowingly or not, live by this motto. It's not something anyone does intentionally or maliciously.

Leadership Buy-In

Typically, learning organizations are pulled in many different directions, and they are juggling such an exorbitant number of learning resources that perspective and direction can get lost in the daily rigor of simply trying to keep up. Making Performance Support a priority in this context is difficult and will need support and backing at every level of the organization. Like any change management initiative, successfully implementing Performance Support involves support from all of the stakeholders involved, especially at the leadership level.

Although leadership may not be the primary consumer of the Performance Support content, they will clearly set the tone for its adoption. As has been discussed throughout this book, many organizations start with a fairly dependent learning culture and one that is not based on a self-service model. There are many variables that need to be supported and reinforced for this discipline to be accepted and internalized. Simply creating great Performance Support solutions is not enough. Without leadership's buy-in and support at every level, these solutions can die before they ever get started.

The two levels of leadership that we have found to be the most critical in supporting the adoption of Performance Support are senior managers and front-line managers. They need to understand and support your PS strategy both financially and culturally. Senior managers play the critical role of setting the overall tone, while front-line managers allow for and support the actual integration and use of PS tools on the job. For this reason, these two groups are often the first stakeholders a learning group needs to deal with when designing a Performance Support framework. The irony of this discipline is that although we have found few leaders who disagree with the overall premise, there are even fewer who understand it at a level that translates into paying for it or supporting its integration into the systems and workflow of the organization. For this reason it is key that a learning organization anticipates the time and effort needed in selling benefits of Performer Support to both of these critical stakeholders.

There are a number of things that can be done in attaining this level of buy-in. The first is to establish a communication strategy that spans the life cycle of each project and the overall strategy. An overall enterprisewide communication strategy will be discussed in greater detail later in this chapter, but for now here are some early steps that should be taken to begin this process.

Buy-in begins with awareness. We have found that providing a series of presentations for each level of management around the merits of a successful Performance Support strategy can go a long way to gaining buy-in and support. Although there are certain key Performance Support principles that will cross all stakeholder groups, it is also important to understand the key business drivers that motivate each in order to elicit the type of support you'll need. All levels need to grasp the key principles of PS and how it complements performance, how it impacts business results, and how it is different from, as well as complementary to, training. Front-line managers will need an additional level of understanding of how PS impacts the daily work performance of their performers and the training programs already offered.

Chapter 1 was written to help you make the case for Performance Support. Table 8.1 outlines the key principles to be shared along with the appropriate target stakeholders. Examples of slides that complement each area can be found at http://performersupport .ning.com/. The measurement issues outlined below will be discussed later in this chapter.

Another critical level of buy-in that needs to be achieved with the front-line managers is their willingness to support and encourage the use of PS back in the workplace. There are two key roles these stakeholders will play in the successful use of PS assets. First, they will need to give their performers time to learn and use these tools. Any new learning asset needs to be taught and internalized. The performer needs to see its value. Adoption will come only through practice and application. As was the case with the calf and the bucket of milk, initially these tools will not be instinctive to the performer, and it will take time for them to be internalized and utilized effec-

Table 8.1. The Key Principles in Making the Case for Performance Support

PS Principle	Stakeholders	Areas to Emphasize
The Changing Performer (Slide 1)	Senior management Front-line management	Leadership needs to understand that their organization is now hosting a very dynamic performer. The question to be addressed is this: Is the current learning culture, and all the assets available to support it, designed to meet the performers' needs? Performance Support is the ideal way to help an organization better address the dynamic performers.
The Knowledge Retention Dilemma (Slide 2)	Senior management Front-line management	Performers journey through two different phases of learning: mastery and competency. *Mastery* is the acquisition of concepts and individual tasks. This type of learning is typically event based, and it can happen either in a classroom or online. *Competency* is the application and integration of concepts and tasks into robust skill sets. It is achieved in the act of performing on the job in the context of work, and it is supported by a Performance Support strategy, related assets, and a well-designed Performance Support tool. The drawback to many learning approaches today is that they are based strictly on a mastery model with little effort or attention given to a competency strategy and related resources. This leads to the retention dropoff shown in the graph in the slide. The orange arrow represents the knowledge impact of complementing a mastery program with Performance Support to enable competency.
The Learning ROI Dilemma (Slide 3)	Senior management Front-line management	Return on investment, or ROI, has been debated in the learning industry for decades. The difficult part of measuring true ROI is looking beyond mastery and quantifying learning's impact on competency. Programs that focus only on mastery are being unfairly held accountable for a level of learning they don't directly impact. To attempt to achieve competency measures from the use of only mastery learning assets is not attainable. If an organization wants to gain business outcomes that lie in competency measures, they need to adopt a broader learning strategy that includes learning assets that support these moments of need. Adding Performance Support to an existing mastery model will achieve and sustain these types of measures.
What Is Performance Support? (Slide 4)	Senior management Front-line management	Clearly everything starts here. Leadership needs to understand what Performance Support is and the outcomes it will achieve. A standard and working definition for Performance Support is key. The reason this slide is fourth in the order is because it builds on all that's been talked about prior to this slide. Once leadership understands the business drivers being supported and the current learning issues they are facing, they can understand and accept an effective definition.

(continued)

The Five Moments of Learning Need (Slide 5)	Senior management Front-line management	An understanding of this principle is critical to the success of any Performance Support strategy. This slide helps outline the five moments of need and puts them into the proper learning context. The arrow represents the fact that many organizations that support only the first two moments often assume that the learning assets introduced here will be adopted and effective in the last three moments. This is not the case. Many formal learning assets are not designed in a way that makes them consumable during the last three moments. They are designed to teach mastery, not support competency. They lack the correct context and structure to be used as Performance Support assets. The good news is that their potential is not entirely lost. As we discussed in Chapter 5, if they are adapted and accessed through a Performance Support broker, these assets can be reused in the final three moments.
PS Learning Tools (Slide 6)	Front-line management	The next two principles typically apply only to the front-line manager. This stakeholder is closely aligned with the business unit and the learning assets available there. This slide outlines the most common Performance Support assets available to performers within organizations. The issue is not the quality or potential of any of these assets. The problem is the quantity and accessibility. Most organizations we have supported have more than enough Performance Support assets, and often too many! Performance Support of some kind already exists throughout the enterprise. What's often missing are a formal strategy, budget, design, implementation, and maintenance approaches that make it as effective as it could be in achieving the business impact outlined in the measurement slide above.
Supporting Both Formal Training and Performance Support (Slide 7)	Front-line management	This final principle brings everything together. This slide is the inverted PS pyramid outlined in Chapter 5. There are three issues that should be emphasized here: 1. There is an instructional difference between how performers want to consume learning assets during training and during Performance Support. 2. Formal assets can be reused in a broker structure. 3. A successful learning strategy or program needs to have both pyramids if they are going to support a performer across all five moments. To not have one or the other is to ignore key moments of need, which will result in an incomplete learning culture and underachieving performer.

tively. There may be instances in which the use of a PS tool may take a greater amount of time to use than the older, less effective way of doing things. Front-line managers need to allow for and encourage this adoption time.

The second critical role the front-line managers play is encouraging the existing support culture to redirect performers back to the new assets and ways of approaching self-directed support. At first these new approaches will seem difficult and foreign to the performers, and they will instinctively fall back on the old support assets and the resources that provided them. This will often involve the use of peers and other internal help resources, such as a help desk, that are perceived as being easier and the path of least resistance. The front-line managers need to encourage and offer incentives to these support resources to buy in to the new approaches and tools, and they need to redirect performers back to the use of the new approaches. They need to send a clear message that the new PS broker and structure need to be followed and reinforced.

The Impact of Performance Support on a Learning Team

Providing PS in the workflow moves the traditional learning and development team into a mission-critical role supporting mission-critical business processes. This is, of course, a new opportunity, and it may also be a new level of responsibility. The criticality of content developed for competency is higher than content designed for mastery due to the nature of when it's consumed. A PS broker supporting insurance claims agents as they're on the phone working on a flood or fire claim is viewed in a completely different light than a workbook introduced during an onboarding class due to its proximity to the actual work being done. Performance Support is about enabling performance, productivity, compliance, and so on. It is about making people, businesses, and their customers more successful. PS is a business solution that also happens to have been developed by the learning group. It is about delivering business solutions.

By extending learning offerings across the Five Moments of Learning Need, learning groups begin developing a closer relationship with their line of business (LOB), and they a have a deeper understanding of their business challenges. PS is allowing learning organizations to offer an additional level of service based on the same requirements. They need to be able to assist their LOBs in integrating PS into the workflow. This may require the learning organization to develop a deeper understanding of business practices across the organization. They need to understand the intersection of business processes, communication and change management, technology, information architecture and management, and performance. It is no longer about publishing a course and then mandating that before people can be released into the work environment, they have to take the course and pass the assessment. With PS the learning organization now needs to act as a business consultant that understands business objectives, the shifts caused by the pending business initiatives, and how to ensure that users are readied for near-term success and long-term adoption and mastery. The learning organization is now acting as a consultant for the entire life cycle of a business initiative and the resulting system or knowledge base. It is much more of a partnership.

In servicing this new partnership, many new roles are emerging within the learning group. Some are simply an extension of existing roles, while others are new opportunities for growth. Here are a few roles we have seen emerge over the past few years as PS has become more mainstream within the learning groups we have worked with:

- **Learning process specialists:** These specialists take a more holistic view of the learning environment in support of a particular project. They work very closely with instructional designers (IDs) to guarantee consistency across the learning experience and all assets created to support it. They make sure that the content in all learning assets is current and relevant. In terms of level, they are one of the highest levels of individual contributors. The role is designed to support the performer's experience across the five moments of need. A sample of this job description is located at http://performer support.ning.com/.

- **PS analysts:** Rather than concentrate on what content is to be developed and how to deliver it, these specialists are responsible for developing a complete learning and support program that ensures higher levels of performance within the organization. The role is focused on relationships and interactions outside of the learning group. It is a type of internal consultant role.

- **Learning and development IT leads:** Over the years instructional development work has become more technically demanding. IT Leads need to adapt to new tools and techniques quickly and on a project-to-project basis. Conceptually and technically, many of the PS authoring tools are more difficult to learn and understand. A new, more technical role is emerging. These specialists lead any effort at connecting learning content to existing systems and tools. They help IT Leads remain current and proficient on the latest technologies. They also help interface with IT departments as these systems are embedded within applications and assets are brokered across backend content repositories. (Note: Leads doesn't mean leader. It means that they lead that area of work for the team. For example, sometimes you have a Lead Programmer or a Lead Engineer.)

- **PS developers:** These specialists need to be able to construct learning in the inverted pyramid construct. They are the IDs who are able to construct a conceptual mental model of content development as it would be consumed at the moment of need. They need to be willing to take risks and try new things. Developers who need someone to give them the "procedure steps" for every task inevitably fail. Those that succeed are looking to provide contextual solutions and not just transform existing documentation or learning content into a deliverable. They are looking at how to deliver a relevant and effective solution to their learners.

Maintenance Strategy

One of the most critical overall services the learning organization will be called on to provide when implementing a PS strategy is to be able to facilitate the ongoing maintenance of this new type of content. Although learning groups have historically been responsible for maintaining content designed for mastery, learning assets that live in the Apply moment of need demand a different level of attention. To facilitate the success of a PS strategy, a rigorous maintenance strategy needs to be implemented. It should focus on keeping the content up-to-date and relevant. In addition, it should remain integrated at the point of need while providing notice to the target audience when something has been added or changed. The strategy should be flexible in that it should handle inputs from multiple sources, including the performers themselves. The strategy should also be adaptable enough to accommodate the changing needs of the organization, and the related technology and associated processes that serve it.

Many learning organizations will already have a maintenance strategy for their existing formal learning assets. The reviews and updates to these assets are often facilitated by the original content owners or IDs, with the assistance of the lines of business, and they typically occur within a predetermined time frame. This method has proven to be successful as it allows for materials to be updated on a scheduled basis with little impact to the performance of the performers. We recommend that, with a few modifications, this same strategy be employed for PS with the greatest focus being frequency of input reviews and updates.

Unlike classroom training materials whose deficiencies can be worked around by the instructor, PS must be accurate at all times to be successful. The reason for the focus on accuracy is that performers will naturally gravitate toward the information that is both most accessible and also able to aid or ensure their success. If PS is accessible but not accurate, they may seek other support methods. Since most PS solutions will be integrated into the real-time workflow, it is vital for this information to be up-to-date and accurate at all times.

It is recommended that learning organizations leverage their existing maintenance strategy as stated above, with reviews of inputs occurring more frequently. Although you should leverage existing prioritization and approval criteria, the review of PS feedback should happen in a rolling manner. If existing content management systems are used to facilitate the current reviews and approvals, it is recommended that the IDs adapt these processes to track this new type of content change. If these types of systems do not exist, a similar software solution can be created. This can be accomplished by using something as simple as a spreadsheet or as complex as a full change management system. Regardless of the system, it will need to be monitored on a weekly or potentially daily basis so that feedback related to PS items can be addressed prior to performers' looking for other means of support. Many of these systems have notification capabilities or inbox views that facilitate immediate and efficient review of items. If not, IDs or other designees will need to manually monitor this information to ensure that all issues are addressed in an appropriate time frame.

To enable this type of strategy, there are three primary areas of focus: content acquisition, deployment, and notification

Note: This maintenance strategy assumes that during the initial design and development stages, the reuse of objects and information has been fully considered and implemented.

Content Acquisition

The most critical component in maintaining any PS strategy is the ability to obtain and/or receive updated information, which can then be incorporated into the solution in a timely manner. The following techniques are recommended to help facilitate the content acquisition as the inputs into the rolling review cycles.

Performer Feedback

Since PS often lives on the desktop or, at minimum, in the workflow, performers need a way to provide feedback on the quality of the information and the usability of the system (or modality). There are a number of strategies for doing this. Regardless of the method chosen, it should reside in close proximity to the PS solution and be as simple to access as possible. Performers will not provide effective feedback if the process is involved, lengthy, or outside of the business context. The following methods are recommended for the various forms of PS solutions:

- All digital forms of Performance Support (for example, brokers, online help) should contain a feedback option within the framework that sends an automated e-mail to a designated e-mail address.
- Digital Performance Support could also contain a link to a community of practice where topic-based feedback can be collected.
- A self-rating system can be made available within the PS framework.
- Paper-based materials should contain an e-mail address or a URL to a feedback form for providing feedback.
- Paper-based materials should also contain a fax number so an associate can directly edit the material and fax the feedback.

Internal Feedback

Feedback should be provided by internal stakeholders, such as instructors, SMEs, and help desks within the LOBs, using any existing feedback systems or taking advantage of feedback functionality similar to the ones outlined in the "Performer Feedback" section above. Existing systems may need to be modified to allow for broader access and new types of feedback based on this particular delivery type.

New Information

A cross-functional team of SMEs from the key content areas should be identified per PS initiative, and it should be engaged to provide new or updated information prior to any changes being released. If the PS solution is brokering any existing assets such job aids, pdf documents, simulations, or e-learning pages, these assets can continue to be maintained using the current maintenance process. If the PS is authored in an authoring environment, this team can be assigned to provide direct maintenance themselves in their area of expertise. In the early stages, a regularly assigned meeting should be scheduled to share best practices and review the maintenance process. It is best to establish periodic (for example, monthly, quarterly) status meetings with the entire group to determine what changes will be made in the next period and how to incorporate this information into the PS solution the day that the changes are implemented across the organization. If it is not feasible to have a standing meeting with an established group, then it will be the responsibility of the ID to establish a consistent routine to acquire information in a less structured (but still effective) manner.

Content Deployment

Once the most current content is gathered, reviewed, edited, and/or created, a content deployment strategy needs to be employed that reintroduces this content back into the learning and performance environment. The deployment of updated content can be done on either a scheduled or an ad hoc basis. This process should be managed because it will assist with the number of notifications going out to the performers, as well as the overall management of the content. At the same time it is imperative that the deployment is not delayed to the point at which it would impact the accuracy of the information accessed by the performers.

Defects

The content deployment of your PS strategy can be divided into two major categories: defects and change requests.

Defects are typically handled through a *defect resolution process* that focuses on resolving reported issues related to inaccuracy of content or incorrect function of technical features. As was mentioned above, these defects can be reported using an existing content management system by modifying or adding certain reporting cycles, categorization types, and input from the appropriate stakeholders. When reported, these items should be categorized and prioritized in a way that ensures they are addressed and deployed in a timely manner. This type of content needs to be handled differently from the current training maintenance cycles. The example defect deployment schedule in Table 8.2 shows how you can manage defects within your PS solution.

KEY

Urgent: There is a defect in the content or PS system, and no workaround exists, or content is not available in the system.

High: There is a defect in content or PS system, and a workaround exists.

Medium: The item is accurate, but it could be better presented to aid the performer in the completion of a task.

Low: The item is accurate, but the user would like information added or changed based on preference.

Change Requests

Change requests can be handled with a similar process using the existing ID to oversee both the prioritization and deployment of the defect resolution and change requests processes. This is the recommended approach because typically resources that are required to fix an issue are also responsible for implementing any new changes. Table 8.3 lists the best practices to process change requests.

Table 8.2. Example of a Defect Deployment Schedule

Level	Response Time	Fix Time	Deployment
Urgent	1 business day	2 business days	3 business days
High	1 business day	3–5 business days	5–10 business days
Medium	1 business day	Requires prioritization	Requires prioritization
Low	1 business day	Requires prioritization	Requires prioritization

Table 8.3. Example of a Change Request Deployment Schedule

Level	Response Time	Development Time	Deployment
Urgent	1 business day	Based on estimated effort	Based on estimated effort
High	1 business day	Requires prioritization	Requires prioritization
Medium	1 business day	Requires prioritization	Requires prioritization
Low	1 business day	Requires prioritization	Requires prioritization

KEY

Urgent: Change is required to content or technical features to support new business processes or update to supported technology.

High: Change would improve access to information or functional experience with immediate and measurable impact to the business.

Medium: Change would improve access to information or functional experience with slight impact to business.

Low: The change is preferential or functional, with no understood business impact.

Based on the tools used to author the PS frameworks, it is recommended that the process developed to push updated content to the work environment require little to no involvement from IT or application personnel. Some PS platforms allow you to push content to a central location, which is then accessed by individuals with network or Internet access. If a person is only intermittently connected to the network, digital PS tools like brokers will need to be able to synchronize updates when the remote workstation is connected to the network. The latter can be done through standard push/pull technologies like MSI packages or through a player utility installed on the end user's desktop. The latter requires less involvement from an IT organization and ensures that updated content is available to users based on when they need it as opposed to when an IT organization is scheduled to push it. For more on how solutions can be deployed, see Technical Deployment.

Notifications of Changes

It is imperative that notifications of changes be timely, accurate, and visible. This will provide the target audience with the information they need, when they need it, and that the audience will be confident that it is up-to-date and accurate. Over time, when managed well, the performers will begin to trust the information. Although it is still a requirement to provide timely, accurate, and visible release information, the approach to how it is sent can change.

We recommend that you communicate based on major and minor releases. A major release would be whenever a new section of content is added, a large volume of updates have been made, and/or structural changes are made that will impact navigation or process changes. Minor releases include changes to a smaller number of existing content items, or the addition of content that does not require structural changes.

For minor releases, communication points within the PS strategy can be used such as a "What's new" section in the digital PS tool. It is also appropriate to post notices of new information in passive environments like portals. For a major release it is recommended, in addition to adding to the "What's new" section, that an e-mail containing line item changes is sent to the stakeholders and targeted performers. Other communication channels outlined in communication section below can also be used for major and minor changes based on their reliability, frequency, and target audience.

Classroom Transformation

We are frequently asked, "Where's the best place to introduce a PS strategy or solution?" The answer is an easy one: in the classroom. As has been mentioned throughout this book, many performers have been taught to be supported rather than to support themselves. The success of your PS strategy depends as much, if not more, on the performers' ability and disposition to accept a new way of supporting themselves as it does on your having designed the correct tools and brokers. PS has to be seen as supporting all five moments of need with the first two typically experienced and supported in the classroom. The performers have also come to view the classroom as a place where they will be introduced to new tools and behaviors. The instructor is in control of the experience and can increase the probability that the PS strategy will be adopted. The power here is that PS is taught in the context of mastery as a critical tool to support them as they journey into competency.

This journey begins by introducing PS early in the communication strategy (outlined later in this chapter). It is then specifically referenced throughout the classroom experience. Consider displaying and distributing job aids as posters and paper-based takeaways that outline the PS tools and brokers. They can be specifically introduced at the start of class and referred to throughout as job aids that are intentionally being taught and used to support the performer. This process can't be left up to chance. The nature of the classroom needs to change from one of achieving mastery to one of preparing for competency.

To accomplish this, organizations should adopt a new design and delivery approach called *Ramp-up/Ramp-down*. This is a content design method and classroom delivery approach based on the premise that performers can and should be taught how to become more independent in their learning, both by how the instructor facilitates the class and by the design of the activities completed there. The graph in Figure 8.1 represents the ramping up and ramping down of two support dynamics in the classroom: the amount of instructor support offered, represented by the left axis and arrow, and the degree to which performers can be self-directed in their learning, represented by the right axis and arrow.

As instructors intentionally begin to ramp themselves out of supporting the students, they simultaneously replace that support with elements from the PS strategy. Notice that the first resources introduced are peers and then ultimately the PS broker. This sequence

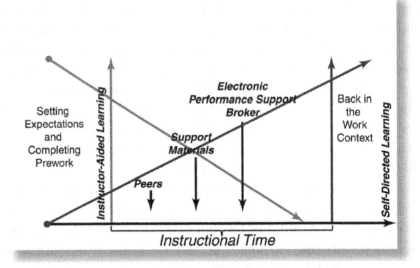

Figure 8.1. The Ramp up/Ramp down Methodology: Preparing Self-Directed Learners

has been designed with the intention of avoiding overwhelming the students. The idea is for students to be able to begin their self-directed journey with familiar and safe resources and to end with the most effective and dependable resources. Also notice that instructors step completely out of supporting the students well before the class ends. This allows performers to practice supporting themselves by using all of the resources taught in class with the instructor present to guide and facilitate. At this critical time, instructors should redirect the students back to the PS tools whenever possible, rather than directly answering questions. This will help the performers gain confidence in their ability to use these tools before they reenter the workplace where the pressures are much greater and the outcomes more important.

Two other aspects of the classroom experience need to be considered in order to help guarantee the success of this approach. The first is the design of the activities being used throughout class. The second is the instructor's ability to facilitate the process.

Activity Design

In a typical mastery classroom, the activities tend to be fairly guiding and instructor centric throughout the experience. These activities need to be modified to accommodate a more guided-to-unguided instructional flow throughout the allotted class time. A *guided activity* will start out by describing a business scenario to be solved, while including steps that walk the performer through solving the problem. Unguided activities are just the opposite. An *unguided activity* is one in which little to no steps or guidance are given in solving the problem. These activities typically contain no more than a scenario describing the business problem to be solved. Using a guided-to-unguided approach across the activities allows the performer to learn to use the PS tools and resources in the context of a safe and supportive environment.

Training the Trainer

Train the trainer for facilitating self-guided learning. Facilitating the Ramp-up/Ramp-down methodology is an unfamiliar approach to many instructors. It's helpful to put in place a Train-the-Trainer program to train instructors how to facilitate this model. The program ought to include opportunities for teach backs, and it should provide guidelines that will help the trainers deliver a consistent learning experience across all the classes being offered. It is critical that each instructor introduces, mentors, and emphasizes the PS framework in the same way.

Technology Considerations

Because PS brokers and other PS assets are IT based, there are a number of technology considerations that need to be addressed if the PS strategy is to be successfully adopted. This section will address the issues to be considered in a successful technical deployment.

Technical Deployment

The goal of the technical deployment is to integrate the PS solution within the intended environment, system or nonsystem. This will enable immediate access to Performance Support items from the workflow and provide support at the moment of need. The necessary items to achieve this goal are dependent on the current assets leveraged, or additional PS tool sets and the environment in which they will provide support. The following section describes best practices for deploying a PS solution independent of specific PS tool sets.

System Deployment

System deployments can be integrated (a) into the technology and/or (b) outside the technology but within the workflow. Often there is a mix of both system and nonsystem tasks contained in these support systems. In any case, here are some best practices for integrating a PS solution into a technology:

- **Context-sensitive linking:** This is accomplished by providing links directly from a system window or page to the corresponding PS object. This would provide the same experience that performers are used to when accessing context-based help systems. Depending on the system this can be integrated into a menu-based system, an existing help link, pressing F1, or all of the above. It is advised to use this method when a performer is using a system to complete most, if not all, of a task. This is the preferred method for most system-based PS solutions.
- **Global links:** This deployment is accomplished by integrating links throughout a system that bring the user to a default location in the PS broker or a more restrictive and traditional help system. These are similar to those accessed from the menu bar of a standard Windows-based application or clicking a global Help link in a Web-based application. In either case, performers are brought to a home page where they can then browse or search for the specific information they require. In some PS

brokers they can navigate through a process or other clickable navigation scheme. It is advised to use this method when procedures are driven by a global process, so it is best used when performers begin at a home page, the majority of the tasks are completed outside of the system, or it is not possible to provide context links.

- **Desktop shortcuts:** This deployment requires the placement of a shortcut to a PS broker on the desktop. It is advised to use this solution in the following conditions: the process or task begins outside of the application, the system is not typically open on a user's workstation and he or she would require support at the initial phases of using the system, and in the event it is not possible to provide inline context or global links.

- **Kiosk applications:** This deployment requires that the digital PS solution be available on a central workstation at all times. For example, think of an airport check-in kiosk. There is a home page or navigation scheme that directs the user in the use of the system. It is advised to deploy this on a shared workstation that supports a specific number of system procedures or even nonsystem procedures that an associate can immediately access.

Measurement Strategies

Throughout this book, we have been extolling the virtues of Performance Support solutions, and we have provided practical advice on how to design and build these solutions. You are now ready to begin your first Performance Support project, and in seeking approval for that first project, you get the question: "How do you know if this is going to work?"

In training, the concept of measuring impact is not a new one. Training departments have been justifying their initiatives and allocated budgets for some time. There are various theories and methodologies that govern training measurement, most notably

Kirkpatrick's Four Levels of Evaluation. So just as building Performance Support solutions will require time and resources, those of us who embark on this journey will have to justify that time and those resources. We should welcome this challenge, however, because by measuring and demonstrating the positive impact of Performance Support solutions and effectively communicating their value, we will gain organizational support.

Measuring the impact of Performance Support solutions is not as difficult as you may think. You can likely use many tools already at your disposal, including those you use to measure formal training or mastery. There is a key differentiator here though: because the data and metrics you will be gathering are at the moment of Apply, they will be more powerful. The usage is directly linked to the workflow, and it is not isolated to the classroom. Then how do we best do this?

The first step in building a measurement strategy is to create an overall framework and a tactical plan for executing. The measurement framework will guide what data is collected and directly affect the overall conclusions on impact. It should be closely aligned with the business objectives of the Performance Support solution—this is why measurement needs to be considered at the beginning of the project. If the decision has been made to build a PS solution, there should be business drivers that influenced that decision. These drivers are the starting point for the measurement framework. Reducing costs could be an objective of a PS solution: by supporting performers at the moment of Apply, organizations can spend less time on costly external resources. Increased productivity could be an objective: reducing the time required to complete a task in an HR system, or reducing the time to competency for new team members attempting to learn call center procedures. A related objective could be to reduce mistakes: decreasing error rates in an accounting system, or minimizing the need for help desk calls to address trivial tasks in a software solution. The objective could be to increase sales, by allowing sales organizations to spend less time learning their customer relationship management (CRM) software and more time closing deals.

The point to be made here is evident. Find those primary business drivers that created the need for the Performance Support solution, and align to those drivers.

The next step is to identify metrics that could already exist in the organization. Taking from some of the examples provided above: Are there help desk metrics that track calls by specific system? Are there metrics on how long it takes a typical call center employee to learn the department's procedures and become productive? Where do errors in the accounting system occur, and when they occur, how much additional work does it create? As much as possible, you should aim to identify existing metrics and data that can be easily obtained.

Once the primary business objectives and measures have been identified, they should become the backbone of your PS strategy. If a key objective of the PS solution was to reduce help desk calls, then certainly a key objective of your measurement efforts should be to show that it did.

Consider now any additional metrics to include in your measurement framework. Typically, you will want to show some evidence of usage and adoption of the PS solution. Of those who have access to the solution, how many are using it? How frequently are they using it? Beyond these simple measures, you may also want to demonstrate the performers' satisfaction with the solution. Are they finding it helpful? Do they perceive that it is impacting their performance? The overall design is certainly a candidate for analysis. Is it well designed? Easy to use? Did it work when it was supposed to?

The business objectives, their related measures, and the additional metrics identified then form the overall framework, in a sense predefining what the end result is going to look like. All stakeholders should know what the measures are and how they will be communicated.

The tactical plan then defines how the measurement study will be executed. Creating the framework was the important first step, but the plan gets down to it. All metrics and measures identified need to be examined. How exactly do you obtain these metrics? Who can provide them? Are they as detailed as you need them to be? Do they actually make sense for what you are trying to say?

What exactly should be measured and when? Here are a few ideas and examples:

Support and Help Desk Calls
- Number of calls
- Types of calls (level 1 versus level 2)
- Length of calls

Sales Numbers
- Sales activity (as captured in CRM software)
- Revenue growth
- Pipeline growth

Productivity Measures
- Errors reported
- Time on task
- Job-specific measures (for example, tasks completed or calls taken)

Cost Reductions
- Time spent in training
- Development time
- Print costs

Usage
- Number of unique users
- Number of repeat users
- Hits (on a Web-based solution)

These are obviously just a few ideas—there are many other potential metrics you can use. Allow those closest to the business process drive what they might be. Keep in mind that the metrics should make sense and demonstrate what you are trying to prove, and it should be possible to gather them easily.

Part of your plan should also include when to collect these metrics. Ideally, you should have a baseline with which to compare the post–PS solution world to the pre–PS solution world. To show that the PS solution had a positive impact on reducing help desk calls, the data should be collected on what the call volume was before the solution was deployed. Comparisons can also be made between similar deployments. How does this HR system upgrade compare to the last HR system upgrade? Demonstrating a positive impact is much easier when a baseline comparison exists. Depending on the PS solution, you may want to gather postdeployment data 30 days out, or up to 90 days out. Allow performers sufficient time to work with the PS solution before gathering data to draw conclusions. Also understand that because PS is not event based, data can be gathered on an ongoing basis to track usage and effectiveness.

Include as many objective, quantitative elements in the measurement plan as possible. They are more difficult to argue and, for many individuals, are the only measures that matter. In addition, consider how to isolate the impact of the PS solution in your plan. For example: A Performance Support solution is rolled out to support a system upgrade. Data shows that fewer errors were made after the rollout. How much of that improvement can be attributed to the PS solution? Oftentimes this can be effectively done through a performer survey.

In fact, performer surveys may end up being a key element of your measurement strategy. They are useful in gathering data on usage, effectiveness, and impact. Of course, when using surveys, it is important to tread carefully and follow some best practices. Ask clear, valid questions that are easy to interpret. Your organization may have standard surveys they use to evaluate training offerings. Start there, and reuse questions that fit. In fact, this allows for a potential opportunity to compare PS solutions to formal training programs. Allow the performers to provide open-ended comments. These comments can shed light on issues that may otherwise have gone unnoticed. Make sure your sample size is large enough to draw reasonable conclusions. Trying to draw conclusions on a performer base of 3,000 with only 50 survey respondents can open up any conclusions for criticism. Also, understand that in surveys there may be a degree of self-reporting bias involved. In other words, the performers have shown a tendency to overreport positive benefits. You may want to account for this self-reporting bias in your findings. A typical correction for this data is usually 25 to 35 percent. For example, performers reported that the PS solution saved them 10 minutes per day that they would otherwise have spent searching for answers. Adjusted by 25 percent, that finding would be reported as 7.5 minutes per day.

As you have seen here, most of the work in building a measurement strategy for Performance Support is done up front—creating the framework, choosing the right measures, and building the plan. With those foundational pieces in place, the only thing left is to execute. Outside of gathering any baseline metrics, the execution of the measurement strategy takes place after deploying the PS solution. At the appropriate times, collect the data: performance metrics, help desk calls, survey results, and so on.

Just as the framework for the measurement strategy was created by starting with the business drivers, any reporting should focus on those drivers. Key business stakeholders may be interested in how many performers are utilizing the solution, but they will be much more interested in seeing whether or not the solution positively affected their organization's performance. Use the overall framework, however, to tell the complete story on impact, usage, adoption, satisfaction, and any other measures you included. The report also provides the perfect opportunity to look at successes, areas of improvement, and potential next projects. The data is there from which to draw these conclusions. A successful measurement strategy will help you show the value of your PS solutions to your stakeholders and to your organization.

HOW TO MAKE IT WORK FOR YOU

Implementing a PS strategy involves many stakeholders. Because PS supports all five moments of need, it will often involve stakeholders in a learning organization who may not be accustomed to working with implementing a PS strategy, and vice versa. In order to anticipate and accommodate everyone who may need to be involved in the many implementation issues outlined in this chapter, we would recommend conducting a stakeholder analysis to be sure all are identified.

Conduct Stakeholder Analysis

A *stakeholder* is defined as anyone who is affected by the PS strategy. One mistake often made when identifying stakeholders is to limit one's attention to include only performers and their direct managers—in other words, those who are the direct consumers of the PS assets. Although they are clearly the stakeholders most affected by the PS strategy, this view does not include all those who will potentially impact its success. For example, we have already outlined the importance of getting buy-in from senior management and of communicating effectively with your internal IT staff. Although both of these stakeholders are not your target audience, they clearly control how well the strategy will be received and maintained.

To guarantee that every stakeholder be involved in the analysis, design, implementation, and ongoing maintenance of a successful PS implementation, we recommend the following steps. (The sample outcome of a stakeholder analysis is shown at http://performer support.ning.com/.)

1. **Identify your stakeholders based on two categories: internal and external.** An *internal stakeholder* is one whose job responsibility falls within the learning organization or who reports indirectly to the learning organization. Examples of stakeholders who would report indirectly might be external vendors or trainers found within the business units themselves. These stakeholders may be directly involved in the PS strategy and would answer to the learning organization relative to this strategy or a particular project, but they would

not be directly linked to the learning organization on any other level. *External stakeholders* are those who fall outside of the learning organization's direct control or reporting structure but who will play a key role in its success. Help desk professionals or IT staffs are often two examples of this type of stakeholder.

2. **Further subdivide these two categories by two levels of impact: first tier and second tier.** Not all stakeholders carry the same degree of importance or impact. Once the stakeholders are grouped into categories, it is important to understand their degree of impact on the overall strategy. *First-tier stakeholders* are critical to the success of the implantation and will receive the highest degree of attention and communication. Although *second-tier stakeholders* are important to the success of the program, their involvement, and the degree to which they need to remain informed, is minimal.

3. **Assign an engagement strategy to each category and tier as appropriate.** Once all stakeholders have been correctly identified and grouped, a unique engagement strategy needs to be identified. Each stakeholder may not warrant its own approach. Some stakeholders, especially those in the second tier, can be grouped based on their level of involvement and impact. The engagement strategy should consider each of the areas outlined in this book: analysis, design, maintenance, and implementation. An overarching communication plan should also be considered across all stakeholders. This approach will be discussed in the next section of this chapter.

Establish a Performance Support Communication Strategy

Like any successful rollout of a given initiative, the degree to which the program is well communicated throughout its life cycle directly impacts its overall success. A well-thought-out and well-implemented communication plan is a final key component of any successful PS strategy.

The recommended communication strategy includes strategic marketing and tactical communication plans to ensure that your stakeholders and target audience receive the appropriate messaging prior to, during, and after your Performance Support solution is available.

Strategic Marketing

The focus of strategic marketing should be a general awareness campaign across both internal and external stakeholders. Prior to the first communication being sent, it is recommended that the PS strategy be assigned a brand to help differentiate it from past training initiatives and assets. This will help to increase the initial exposure and generate interest because people generally respond well to the "packaging" of a solution. This campaign should be released in a staged approach.

The first stage of branded communications should be delivered to the internal learning-and-development (L&D) first-tier stakeholders. This message should focus on the instructional and business benefits of a self-service support framework. This will begin to not only build awareness but it will also assist the change management process related to how learning and support will be developed in the future.

The second phase of the strategic marketing plan should focus on the external first-tier stakeholders. This message should follow the tone of the prior message, but it should be more specific to the business benefits of the cultural shift to a support framework geared more to self-service. These messages should be delivered in conjunction with the release of each initial pilot and learning program.

It is important to note that the brand and related message should be specific to the current business culture and relevant to the target audience, and they should be bold enough not to become muted by other initiatives. For this reason, the rollout of other organizationally critical nontraining programs should also be considered.

The strategic marketing plan should be an ongoing campaign with perpetual messaging using the most appropriate publishing cycle for the stakeholders. It should be delivered across the communication channels that exist throughout the enterprise. An additional communication plan should be considered that collects and shares the successes and feedback of each program throughout its life cycle. For example, a performer-driven self-rating system can be very helpful with self-marketing. This information should be both anecdotal and mapped to qualitative and quantitative measures.

Tactical Communications

Beyond an overall branding and PS awareness campaign, each initial pilot and program will need its own tactical communication plan promoting the value of the PS solution and its most effective use in the workplace. The learning team should consult with each LOB regarding communication and assist in providing PS-specific messaging and collateral that emphasize how PS can be utilized to increase the performers' ability to effectively and efficiently complete their job tasks while increasing overall satisfaction and reducing support requirements. The more this message pivots on specific needs and projected benefits, the higher the return and usage. Focus groups can be conducted prior to the creation of LOB-specific communication plans to help better tailor the plan.

The tactical plan should include communications targeted at two audiences: overall stakeholders and performers.

Both internal and external key stakeholders should receive ongoing tactical communications on the progress and impact of each PS initiative. Internal stakeholders should receive information specific to the design, implementation, and effectiveness of the program, including items such as the number of deliverables produced, the business impact of these deliverables, and feedback on design and implementation issues. The external stakeholders need to receive similar messages, but the messages should pivot more on business metrics than on design. Metrics such as time to completion, use of the PS system, time spent in the workflow versus time spent in training or accessing a training asset such as e-learning, and reduced support requirements would be potential focus areas.

When a formal PS framework is not assigned to a learning project, aligned with business outcomes, and validated by its impact on the work environment, PS is misunderstood as yet another training resource. PS needs to be communicated to the stakeholder groups in terms of its impact on efficiencies and productivity. When learning solutions containing PS components are proposed, the communication should highlight the following specific benefits:

1. The time in training is shortened because the associates can now acquire more information on the job and do not require as much time in class.

2. The impact and effectiveness of a system rollout or nonsystem program can be measured through metrics such as time to competency and/or proficiency, time to resolution, number of calls to a help line, or the amount of time spent with a coach or other SME.

Communications with Performers

Performers should be specifically targeted for ongoing tactical communications. Since most organizations do not have a learning environment that centers on self-service, messaging will need to reinforce the value and effectiveness of the PS brokers, the tools associated, and the path through the assets. The PS strategies taught in class need to be constantly reinforced at the performer level and in the context of the workflow. The ongoing tactical communications should be modified based on learner feedback and utilization numbers. Also, any positive metrics and anecdotes should be shared as well.

INSIGHTS FROM A THOUGHT LEADER: Carol Stroud

Carol Stroud, *a performer support consultant, works with medium- to large-sized organizations to help them transition from a traditional corporate training method to a more comprehensive learning and Performance Support approach. The PS approach includes the implementation of appropriate learning technologies, as well as formal and informal learning strategies, to support the full spectrum of front-line staff performer support needs.*

Stroud has a master of distance education degree, with a specialization in e-learning. She has worked in the field for over 10 years, acquiring considerable experience from corporate, academic, health care, and not-for-profit settings. She represents the professional for whom this book is written.

A View from within the Workflow

I became a bad corporate e-learner after years of frustration with the results of traditional e-learning. When I had to take e-learning as part of a job requirement, I did what I needed to do to get through the evaluation process—usually a set of multiple-choice questions. In one situation, I was tasked with completing almost eighty 20-minute lessons that made up a corporate e-learning package on a piece of software that supported a business process.

After the first few lessons, I figured out that I didn't actually need to complete the reading-interactive components of the e-learning. All I had to do was go over and over the end-of-lesson quizzes until I got all the answers correct. I did this by writing down my answers and then, through a process of elimination, figuring out how to correct the answers I got wrong. The end result was that I met the corporate requirement for taking the training—all my lessons were marked "completed" in the learning management system. But for the life of me, I couldn't use the application that I was supposed to have learned by taking the training. If I was responding this way to the traditional corporate e-learning package (and I clearly should have known better . . .), what value was that package really bringing to the organization? Is there a better way? If there is a better way, what does it look like?

I discovered Performance Support, Bob and Conrad, and their work through the Internet. I learned about the Five Moments of Learning Need and all the concepts and more that have been discussed in this book by attending workshops, seminars, and other events. Their ideas made perfect sense, and they put all the different pieces of the performer support picture into their right places.

Learning theories and concepts is one thing; implementing them in the real world is something else! As a student of Performance Support, and as a member of the target audience for this book, I would like to share with you a few of my PS lessons learned.

If You Don't Know Where You Are Going, Any Road Will Take You There

Performance Support solutions need to enable organizational goals and objectives. This seems like a flash of the obvious. However, I have encountered many situations in which decisions were made to enter into learning and/or training solutions that were quite disconnected from the real needs of the organization. Decisions were influenced by things like opportunities (buying a particular technology that drives a corporate learning solution as part of a larger purchase in an effort to achieve economies of scale) or pressures from deadlines (where there was no time to go through a thoughtful requirements-gathering and decision-making process). The result was a lot of wasted time, effort, and money expended by the organization on so-called solutions that completely missed the mark.

Performance Support solutions are people solutions. On one project, I was brought in to develop an e-learning solution similar to a previous e-learning solution that had, by all accounts, failed. Further investigation revealed the e-learning material was separate from the Web-based tool it was meant to support. Users were busy, and they chose to not complete the e-learning material that explained how to use the Web-based tool. Instead, users went directly into the Web-based tool and quickly became frustrated with the lack of usability of this component that was critical to one of their business processes.

The ripple effect from the lack of usability, and hence user buy-in, was significant. The target audience abandoned the use of the Web-based tool in sufficient numbers to derail a critical business process, which in turn undermined the achievement of organizational goals and objectives. By paying attention to users' requirements and their experiences, more performer support was embedded into the tool itself along with a smaller e-learning package that focused on showing how to use the performer support resources. Usability and user buy-in improved significantly, the business process flowed more smoothly, and organizational goals and objectives were now in reach. Had a single e-learning solution been pursued yet again, failure would most likely have been the outcome.

Develop a Grounding Framework

PS concepts and principles must be framed by organizational context as the first step to achieving key stakeholder buy-in, and thus organizational change. I do this by presenting an overall Learning and Performance Support framework, adapted from Marc Rosenberg, *Beyond e-Learning (2007)*, that shows how learning and performance support resources can be made available to performers in an organization. The channels include both formal and informal learning environments and use different delivery methods such as these:

- Formal learning options (outside the normal workflow)
- On-site classroom
- Online learning
- Informal learning options (converged within the workflow)
- Performance support resources and tools
- Mentoring and coaching
- Information repositories
- Organizational experts and expertise
- Communities of practice and networks

My key talking points include these:

1. **Not all learning takes place in a classroom.** Both formal learning and informal workplace settings are identified. Research has indicated that only a small portion (10 to 20 percent) of what is learned in a classroom is actually transferred to the job. Research has also indicated that overall, approximately 80 percent of learning takes place informally on the job. Leaders in the PS industry suggest the use of a Knowledge Transfer Rule when supporting people in the workplace, where 10 percent of learning is done in a formal setting, 20 percent is done through mentoring and coaching, and the final 70 percent occurs through PS resources and tools.

2. **Not all learning requires an instructional solution.** Instructional solutions are considered to be "push learning" whereas performer support solutions are considered to be "pull learning." According to Rosenberg (2007), "push learning" occurs when the content is defined, developed, and delivered to a staff member in a formal setting. "Pull learning" occurs when the staff member has the resources available and is self-motivated to use them to help in the performance of his or her job.

The framework also provides an opportunity to acknowledge the relevant work completed by the organizational learning team, which paves the way for new ideas. The framework highlights that a single option alone, such as e-learning, will not be enough to meet user and organizational needs and that several options are available to develop a comprehensive approach to providing performer support.

The framework is synchronized with the Five Moments of Learning Need. When working with people who are new to the concepts of performer support, I start by identifying which of the five moments of need are to be addressed. Then we turn to the framework to look at different options available for delivering the information to meet those needs. Using the framework and the five moments of need together gives people a concrete way to see how they are currently doing business and what other options are available beyond the standard organizational response (for example, classroom training) for meeting the five moments of need. It also provides the opportunity to show that current ways of doing business won't go away; they will continue to be used, but they will be optimized to more effectively support learners' and organizations' needs.

Connecting the Pieces Together through Business Process Backbone

I have yet to work with an organization that was not trying to implement multiple, enterprise-wide initiatives concurrently using the same staffing mix. The challenge is to connect the work of the different initiatives so that they make sense and are manageable to those people who are tasked with implementing them.

The key to making these connections is the well-defined business processes that results from the *rapid task analysis* (RTA). A well-defined business process provides a strong backbone upon which connections can be made to the work of different systemwide initiatives. As well, a Performance Support infrastructure is an ideal way to link legislative and accreditation requirements to daily workflow.

The culture of an organization can, and usually does, result in strong resistance to participating in a rapid task analysis. In these cases it can take several months of work to achieve buy-in to the point of acceptance of the RTA process. Being able to clearly articulate how defining the business processes can help to connect the strategic initiative work together to the benefit of the front-line staff and to the organization overall is an important key message for helping to achieve the required stakeholder buy-in.

People, Process, and Technology: A Change Management Challenge

Implementing a PS framework involves changing three interconnected elements of the enabling infrastructure: process, people, and technologies. Change one element in the triangle, and the other two elements must be addressed as well. The other elements must be evaluated to make sure that an optimized balance is maintained so that organizational goals can be achieved efficiently, effectively, and within the financial constraints of the business environment.

A change management strategy will be required to address the impact of change across the enterprise. Yet, in most organizations change management is not part of the skill set of the learning team. Experience is teaching me that this should change. Along with learning about the theories, benefits, and how to implement Performance Support, PS specialists should be knowledgeable and skilled in navigating organizations through the high degree of change they will encounter as they move into PS strategy implementation. In large organizations, a dedicated *PS governance mechanism* may be needed. This issue on its own is worthy of a dedicated article!

Conclusion

My intent in this article has been to share a few of my insights into the reality of implementing a PS solution in medium to large organizations. My early experiences with developing, implementing, and using conventional e-learning materials resulted in my search for a better way. The better way manifested itself in Bob and Conrad's Performance Support and the Five Moments of Learning Need because this approach, in my experience, is better aligned with the needs of the key stakeholders in this equation—the end users. Taking care of the end users' moments of learning needs will set the organization on the path to achieving its goals and objectives.

Endnotes

Chapter 1

1. Eric Hoffer (1902–1983), U.S. philosopher, *Reflections on the Human Condition*, aph. 32 (1932, 1973).
2. McKinsey & Company, www.mckinseyquarterly.com/The_new_normal_2326.
3. See www.emc.com/collateral/analyst-reports/expanding-digital-idc-white-paper.pdf. See also Kathleen Parker, "Turn Off, Tune Out, Drop In," *Washington Post*, December 2008, www.washingtonpost.com/wp-dyn/content/article/2009/03/31/AR2009033103318.html.
4. Martin Joerss and Henry Zhang, "A Pioneer in Chinese Globalization: An Interview with CIMC's President," *McKinsey Quarterly*, May 2008.
5. See "Compete and Collaborate: What Is Success in a Connected World?" 11th Annual Global CEO Survey, PriceWaterhouseCoopers, 2008, p. 36. The study notes that the "ability to adjust to internal and external changes quickly" is considered a critical skill by 80 percent of the CEOs surveyed.
6. See "Unlocking the DNA of the Adaptable Workforce: The Global Human Capital Study 2008," IBM Global Business Services, p. 28. The "inability to rapidly develop skills to address current/future business needs" is cited as the "primary workforce-related issue facing organizations." See also Christopher G. Worley and Edward E. Lawler III, "Designing Organizations That Are Built

to Change," *MIT Sloan Management Review,* vol. 48, no. 1, Fall 2006, p. 19.

7. PriceWaterhouseCoopers, 10th Annual Global CEO Survey, January 2007, p. 11.

8. See https://secure3.verticali.net/pg-connection-portal/ctx/noauth/Portal-Home.do.

9. Edgar H. Schein, "How Can Organizations Learn Faster? The Challenge of Entering the Green Room," *MIT Sloan Management Review,* vol. 34, no. 2, Winter 1993, p. 90.

10. Our point of view is that a fruitful vein of future research will explore the relationship between learning and leadership in the context of developmental stages theory, such as Robert Kegan's six equilibrium stages. See Robert Kegan, *The Evolving Self,* Harvard University Press, Cambridge, 1982.

Chapter 3

1. G. A. Miller, "The Magical Number Seven, Plus or Minus Two: Some Limits on Our Capacity for Processing Information," *Psychological Review,* vol. 63, 1956, pp. 81–97.

2. J. Sweller, J. J. van Merrienboer, and F. G. Paas, "Cognitive Architecture and Instructional Design," *Educational Psychological Review,* vol. 10, 1998, pp. 251–257.

3. R. E. Mayer, *Multimedia Learning,* 2nd edition. Cambridge University Press, Cambridge, United Kingdom, 2009.

4. R. C. Clark and R. E. Mayer, *E-Learning & the Science of Instruction,* 2nd edition, Wiley, San Francisco, 2008, pp. 148–171.

5. R. E. Mayer, *Multimedia Learning.*

6. J. Sweller, P. Chandler, P. Tierney, and M. Cooper, "Cognitive Load and Selective Attention as Factors in the Structuring of Technical Material," *Journal of Experimental Psychololgy: General,* vol. 119, 1990, pp. 176–192.

7. R. E. Mayer, *Multimedia Learning.*

Chapter 4

1. http://thinkexist.com/quotation/champions_know_that_success_is_inevitable-that/262103.html..

Chapter 6

1. Henry Jenkins, "Critical Information Studies for a Participatory Culture (Part One)," www.henryjenkins.org/2009/04/what_went_wrong_with_web_20_cr.html.

Index

About the Authors

Conrad Gottfredson has a Ph.D. in Instructional Psychology and Technology with over 25 years of experience helping multinational organizations in their leadership development, performance improvement, learning agility, instructional design, and knowledge capital management. His consulting work has helped clients wisely employ emerging technologies and methodologies to help people achieve personal and organizational goals. He has pioneered methodologies for developing and delivering learning at the "Five Moments of Need" to those who need it, when they need it, in the language and form they require, from a single source of content. His unique collaborative consulting style has helped him develop simple, practical solutions to the common challenges facing organizations at all levels.

Bob Mosher has been an active and influential leader in the learning and training industry for over 25 years and is renowned worldwide for his pioneering role in e-learning and new approaches to learning. Bob is currently the Global Chief Learning and Strategy and Evangelist with a leading role in LearningGuide's international management team. He joined LearningGuide from Microsoft, where he was Director of Learning Strategy and Evangelism. Before, Bob was the Executive Director of Education for Element K where he directed and influenced their learning model and products. He is an influential voice in the IT training industry, speaking at conferences and participating within industry associations.